William H. H. Murray

Daylight Land

The Experiences, Incidents, and Adventures, humorous and otherwise, which befel

Judge John Doe, Tourist, of San Francisco

William H. H. Murray

Daylight Land
The Experiences, Incidents, and Adventures, humorous and otherwise, which befel Judge John Doe, Tourist, of San Francisco

ISBN/EAN: 9783337192327

Printed in Europe, USA, Canada, Australia, Japan

Cover: Foto ©ninafisch / pixelio.de

More available books at **www.hansebooks.com**

"OUT OF THE WHITE BLANKNESS STARTED LETTERS RED AS BLOOD."
See page 293.

DAYLIGHT LAND

The Experiences, Incidents, and Adventures, Humorous and Otherwise, which befel Judge JOHN DOE, *Tourist, of San Francisco;
Mr.* CEPHAS PEPPERELL, *Capitalist, of Boston; Colonel*
GOFFE, *the Man from New Hampshire, and divers
others, in their Parlor-Car Excursion over
Prairie and Mountain*

ALL OF WHICH I SAW, AND ONE OF WHOM I WAS

As recorded and set forth by

W. H. H. MURRAY

ILLUSTRATED WITH ONE HUNDRED AND
FORTY DESIGNS IN COLORS

UNDER THE SUPERVISION OF

J. B. MILLET

BOSTON
CUPPLES AND HURD
MDCCCLXXXVIII

To

GEORGE STEWART, Jr., D.C.L., D. Litt., F. R. G. S.

OF QUEBEC

WHO HAPPILY REPRESENTS

THE BEST THAT THERE IS IN CANADIAN CULTURE AND CHARACTER

I DEDICATE

IN EVIDENCE OF MY ESTEEM AND ADMIRATION

THIS VOLUME

THE AUTHOR

CONTENTS.

Chap.		Page
	Introduction	17
I.	The Meeting	23
II.	At Breakfast	29
III.	A Very Hopeful Man	42
IV.	The Big Nepigon Trout	53
V.	The Man in the Velveteen Jacket	68
VI.	The Capitalist	95
VII.	A Jolly Camp at Rush Lake	121
VIII.	Big Game	139
IX.	A Strange Midnight Ride	167
X.	Banff	183
XI.	Nameless Mountains	211
XII.	Sabbath among the Mountains	224

CONTENTS.

Chap.		Page
XIII.	The Great Glacier	258
XIV.	The Hermit of Fraser Cañon	274
XV.	Fish and Fishing in British Columbia	298
XVI.	Vancouver	307
XVII.	The Parting at Victoria	326

LIST OF ILLUSTRATIONS.

FROM DESIGNS BY J. D. WOODWARD, J. C. DURAND, C. BROUGHTON, C. COPELAND, J. CARTER BEARD, C. H. JOHNSON, AND OTHERS.

	PAGE
"OUT OF THE WHITE BLANKNESS STARTED LETTERS RED AS BLOOD"	*Frontispiece*
VERMILION LAKES	9
THE JUDGE	10
THE THREE SISTERS, CANMORE	11
"A SCHOLARLY LOOKING MAN"	15
A VOICE FROM THE DOORWAY	17
"I GO AS A PILGRIM"	18
"THOU SHALT WRITE US"	21
THE BOW RIVER, NEAR CALGARY	23
INITIAL LETTER	23
"OUR HANDS MET LIKE A FLASH"	24
ON THE ROAD TO THE GLACIER	25
"HOW FRESH THE LADIES LOOK"	28
JACKFISH CROSSING, LAKE SUPERIOR	29
INITIAL LETTER	29

LIST OF ILLUSTRATIONS.

"Count the clicks"	30
The Waiter	31
The First Bridge	33
The Rope Bridge	35
Caribou Road Bridge, Fraser River	37
A Real Gem	39
Red Rock and Nepigon Bay	41
Thunder Cape, Lake Superior	42
Initial Letter	42
Crowfoot Encampment	45
The Judge glared	48
"Dynamite is n't so bad, after all"	52
Griffin Lake, Eagle Pass	53
Initial Letter	53
Civilization means luxury	54
Fraser Cañon, above Spuzzum	57
"Jerusalem! He's a twenty-pounder"	63
On the Columbia River	67
Salmon Cache	68
Initial Letter	68
Mt. Carroll, from the West	71
The Hackman	79
The Runaway Colt	87
"The dog and cat met"	91
A Miner's Hut	94
Mt. Mackay, near Port Arthur	95
Initial Letter	95
"I am delighted to greet you"	97
"Busted, completely busted"	102
Black Cañon	103
"He followed me"	105
Goats' Heads	106
"On a cliff, stood Percussion"	107
Goats' Heads	109
The Path of the Avalanche	111
The Man of Science	115
A Trial of Strength	116

LIST OF ILLUSTRATIONS.

"He struck the man of science"	120
Near Revelstoke	121
Initial Letter	121
Jack Osgood	123
Primitive Transportation	125
Indian Girl	131
The Man from New Hampshire	135
Kananaskis Falls	138
The Mountain Lion	139
Initial Letter	139
Gray Wolf	140
White Tail Deer	141
Buffalo	144
White Fox	146
Musk Ox	148
Prong Horn Antelope	149
Caribou	152
Rocky Mountain Goat	154
Rocky Mountain Sheep	157
The Grizzly Bear	161
Moose	163
Sea Otter	166
Bow River and Cascade Mountains, near Banff	167
Initial Letter	167
In the Selkirks	169
Kicking Horse Pass	176
Sapomaxicow, Chief of Blackfeet	179
Falls of the Bow, Banff	183
Initial Letter	183
The Bow River, Banff	187
Mt. Stephen, and Glacier, and Cathedral Mountain	191
Fraser Cañon, below North Bend	197
Vermilion Lakes	208
On the Tote Road	209
Van Horne Range	211
Initial Letter	211
Albert Cañon	215

LIST OF ILLUSTRATIONS.

Cathedral Peak	217
Mt. Field	222
Ruby Creek	223
Hermit Range	224
Initial Letter	224
"There comes our clergyman"	225
Ross Peak	229
A Mountain Picnic	237
East Ottertail	245
The Chancellor	253
Great Glacier from the Snow Sheds	258
Initial Letter	258
Climbing the Great Glacier	260
The Great Glacier	261
Mt. Hermit, Rogers Pass	265
Sir Donald	271
Mt. Stephen, from the East	273
Kicking Horse Lake, Hector	274
Initial Letter	274
Caribou Wagon Road, Fraser Cañon	276
Eagle Peak	277
Symbols and Figures	282
"On the rock was a letter 'C'"	285
Indian Burying Ground	288
Bow River	297
Chinook Indians	298
Initial Letter	298
Hope Peaks	300
Castellated Cliffs, Ashcroft	302
Salmon Drying	304
Drying Candle Fish	305
Kamloops Lake	307
Initial Letter	307
Tossing for Corner Lots	309
Panoramic view from Vancouver	312, 313
Cedar Tree, Vancouver Park	315
Spruce Tree, Vancouver Park	319

LIST OF ILLUSTRATIONS. 15

The Ball	323
Indian Chief's Grave	325
Pitt River	326
Initial Letter	326
Siwash Canoes	327
An Old Squaw	330
Medicine Man	330
Indian Hermit	331
Squaw of the Medicine Man	331
At New Westminster	332
Flathead Indians	334
The Parting	335
At the Station	338

INTRODUCTION.

Speed the going guest.

"WHITHER art thou going, O wanderer, this summer?" said a pleasant voice from the doorway, as I came up the gravel walk. "Are you going to the North and the home of ice, or to the East and the gates of the morning? Or do you long for the odor of tropical flowers and the flash of colored wings? Or shall you voyage to the West, that land of old-time fable, in which the blessed lived? Tell me, thou ranger of woods, with thy whitened head and the heart of a boy, whither goest thou this summer?"

"I am going, fair princess," I said, imitating the lightness of her phrasing, — "I am going to the West, to that heaven of the old-time folk, where the colors on the clouds are as golden as thy hair, and the sky as blue as thine eyes. I am going to the West, fair princess, where the plains are of emerald, the mountains snow-crowned, and the streams flow yellow with gold."

"How goest thou, O wanderer?" continued the voice banteringly from the doorway. "Has Phœbus loaned you his car and taught you the government of his steeds? Beware! Remember the fate of Phaeton! Or has the sea sent you word that the Dolphins are

waiting, all harnessed to the bowl of the pink pearl shell? Or do you go like a true pilgrim, with sandalled foot and scalloped shoon? Is it by the poetry or prose of power that you are to be drawn?"

"By both," I responded. "The fate of Phaeton has warned me, and the pearly shell car of the Dolphins is small. I go as a pilgrim, but a pilgrim favored by the gods. I have sandals, and I shall walk when I choose. I have wings, — wings like an eagle's, and I shall fly where I will. And whether I fly or walk, I shall go with eyes open."

"'I!' You surely go not alone!"

"Ay, alone," I responded, — "alone with my thoughts and my fancies, an endless train of companions."

"But surely thou shouldst take one friend at least for the night, one comrade for the trail?"

"Sweet spirit," I rejoined, "the cheerful face, the courteous tongue, the open hand, the honest heart, find friends where'er they go. All camp-fires shine for such, all doors fly open at their coming. The listening ear finds voice of knowledge, and for the seeing eye God paints his pictures everywhere. He who takes humor with him has princely entertainment with a crust, and mirthfulness laughs the long road short. The young need company beyond themselves, but with the whitened head come thoughts which make companionship."

"O wise philosopher!" exclaimed the voice more soberly, "hast thou a charm against danger and an amulet for ill? Dost thou not fear to leave the loved behind?"

"He who loves takes all his loved ones with him where'er he goes," I answered. "Even their cares and wants abide with him, and the air which is forever round him on all sides is as a polished mirror to reflect their faces. Love owns imagination, and in it as a constant sky she sees forever all her stars fast fixed."

"If we may not go with thee, dear one," she answered, "then our conspiracy must be uncovered. Each year thou leavest us — it is thy habit, and for weeks we have mistrusted thee. Hence we have counselled — we of thy hearth and heart — and plotted lovingly, and I am spokeswoman of the plot. We have decided we will not let you go unless you give us solemn promise."

"Promise? I will promise anything — on such an altar swear at random. Bring out the household. You are all rogues alike, for they come quickly at your signal, — too quickly to be honest. Now see I such sweet tyrannies as never blessed a kingdom. Who could resist? I promise to obey."

[She reads.] "We of thy house do hereby agree to let thee go a-journeying again, and grant thee liberty to be gone for many weeks or months, as seemeth to thee good, — provided, that of all lovely sights, of all beautiful things and places that thou seest, of all strange people and uncouth objects, of all happy days and farcical conceits, along with all humorous incidents and mirthful experiences, thou shalt write us a full and faithful account. And if in journeying thou meetest with clever folk, with men and women gifted with mother-wit to make thee laugh, what they say shall be writ down for us, that we who bide here while thou farest on may not be lonely, but share with thee the profit and entertainment thou dost meet with. So shall this journey of thine be a happy one in truth, to all of us, and all the days be winged until we meet again. Dost thou promise?"

"Ay, ay," I answered briskly. "The yoke that Love lays on us is easy and the burden light. My pen shall keep pace with my feet. For your delight I will be tourist and scribbler both. You shall see what I see, — rivers and plains, mountains and snowy peaks, sunrises and sunsets, with all their glow, and starry nights, the works of men, and the nobler works of God. And what I hear to stir my mirth I will send you fairly written out; so shall your laughter be as echo to my own. And now the stirrup-cup. I drain it to safe-keeping of the house. We'll have sweet meeting after many days."

"THOU SHALT WRITE US."

DAYLIGHT LAND.

CHAPTER I.

THE MEETING.

Welcome, old friend! A hundred thousand welcomes.

"THOU art the man!" cried a voice behind me, as I stepped out of the bathroom, prepared for the pleasures of the day as only a man can be by a bath,—"thou art the man, or my eyes are blind, or the man that trailed that dreadful trail of the Staked Plains with me has a double."

"Judge Doe!" I cried, and our hands met like a flash. "Not a man on the earth would I sooner see at this minute than yourself. This magnificent room"— and I glanced at the elegant car — "is not much like the spot where we made our first meeting." And I thought of that barren waste of sand where I ran across him, without guide or water, as he wandered half blinded under the awful heat. "Do you remember the canteen I gave you, and how you swore that the half boiling water in it was as cold as iced sherbet?" And I laughed at the memory.

"And so it was," returned the Judge stoutly. "At least, so it seemed at that moment, and of one thing I am certain, that that drink from your old canteen saved my life."

"I shouldn't wonder," I replied. "For if you had not had it when you did you would probably have been wandering a madman over the sands in half an hour. But a fig to the Staked Plains and the old memories! We are here in this car, with plenty to eat and drink; and so tell me, where are you going?"

"I am going home to the Golden Gate," he replied, "and I have come clean up from Washington to take this route. I wanted to escape the dust and the heat

THE MEETING. 25

of more southern ones, the alkali plains, and the hot looking ochred cañons and the Buttes, which are all right in winter, but which in midsummer make me feel, as the train rolls down into them, as if I were being pushed into the mouth of an oven. An old friend told me in Washington that I could reach San Francisco this way without the alkali dust, the infernal heat, and the glaring red colors, ride four hundred miles between glaciers, and see such scenery as I never saw on the Continent, and so I am here. But where are you going, old comrade of hot Texan trails and arid Arizona? Are you, too, bound for the Blessed Isles lying under the sunset?"

"Ay, ay," I returned laughingly, and in the same light strain that the Judge had taken. "I too am going to the West; not the West of classic fable, but of modern fact. I go, not to reach home, nor escape dust and heat, but to see the great mountains between the prairies and the sea. I met John Carrol at Parker's, in Boston, last week, — you remember Carrol, the man we met among the Nevadas that summer? — and he told me that the Canadian scenery was beyond description; that I could ride three hundred miles along glacial streams, with the glaciers from which they flow in full sight, with hundreds of mountains, that have not even been named, rising ten thousand feet above the level of the track; and knowing him to be careful of statement, I packed my valise, and here I am."

"Here I am, too, for about the same reason," said a quiet voice behind me, and a hand stole slyly into mine; and looking around, there was Colonel Goffe, or, as we facetiously called him during the journey, "the Man from New Hampshire."

"You see," he continued, after I had presented him to the Judge, "I own a ranch somewhere among the foot-hills beyond Calgary, and my oldest boy is making his start in life on it. He has been out there two years, and I thought I would run over and see how he is getting along. He is to meet me at some station near the ranch, and is to go through with me to the coast, for he wrote that he did not wish me to see even the ranch until I had seen the mountains, the glaciers, and the great forests."

How delightful, often, are the surprises of travel! To think that, coming from different parts of the world, after years of wandering, without knowledge of each other's movements or purposes, we two, who had parted years before in Arizona, should meet face to face in this palace car, travelling for almost the same purpose, and with the same object in view, and that we old trailers, who had so often bivouacked together, and shared the same blanket, should have slept all night within a few feet of each other, not knowing! Are the meetings of life accidental, or is there a Power above us which arranges and compels the meetings and partings of our lives?

"This is going to be a happy journey," said the Judge pleasantly, as he looked at the passengers grouped here and there. "I can see it in their faces. Bless me, how fresh the ladies look! There is not a tired face in the car."

Dear old happy-hearted Judge! I wonder if the prophecies of men are not born of their moods, after all? For with all thy nice taste and delicate sense of the fit and the needful, never did I meet a lighter heart or a happier disposition than thine.

But indeed it was a rare company, for it was wholly composed of intelligent and refined people, accustomed to travel, and travel-wise. And best of all, we were filled with curiosity and some of us with incredulity touching the wonders it had been foretold us we should see, — such marvels and majesties of nature as in truth make the ride from Calgary to Vancouver like a journey through fairy and giant land.

Thus, with old friends unexpectedly met; with a throng of bright and courteous people around us, and feeling that we were a " goodly companie going to seek goodly things," our happy journey, as the dear old Judge had prophetically called it, began.

CHAPTER II.

AT BREAKFAST.

A feast of reason and a flow of soul.

"TAKE another cup of this delicious coffee, Judge," I said to my companion at the table. We are travelling like the gods, and it is fit that we should fare like the gods.

"Your conceit is a happy one," replied the Judge, as he inspected his cream. "This is the true nectar of Olympus, if it was drawn from the udder of a cow. The ancients hit it exactly. Their heaven was only the sublimating of the earth. Their goddesses were their best-looking women, their gods crowned athletes, and their Parnassus nothing but an idealized summit of a hill in Attica. We moderns separate our heaven from the earth, and so lose the beautiful sequence of the divine plan. If in the place of theologians we had the old sages again, our children would be taught the sweet lesson that the heavenly is only

the earthly in bloom, and that angels are but men and women who have been educated a little higher up than the schooling of this life carries them."

"And you might add," I suggested, "that this manner of travel which we are now enjoying is only a modern method of flying."

"Certainly," said the Judge, as he buttered his roll, "we are flying. Count the clicks," — and he held up his watch, — "forty in twenty seconds; that gives us the number of miles to the hour. Forty miles an hour and at breakfast! Could an angel keep her stroke with a cup of coffee in her hand? See! the liquid does n't sway in the cup. I wonder if the navvies that made this road-bed appreciated their work?"

"The passengers do, if they did n't," I responded, "and that is the important thing, perhaps. The bee may not know the sweetness of its own honey nor the mathematical perfection of its cell. But the man gifted with the delicacy of taste and the artistic sense appreciates both. The lower order does the work and the higher one gives the applause. That seems to be the way of it."

At this moment we went roaring over a bridge whose mighty span stretched in majesty a hundred feet above the mad water that poured whirling downward below us. We glanced from the window as the rumbling gave us its signal, and our mind received this photographic impression: A mountain to the right, mounded like a loaf, and wooded perfectly from base to dome; to the left a precipice, lifting sheer half a thousand feet from the dark pool lying sullen and black in its shadow; through this gorge and beyond, in the distance, a space of sky shone like a mirror, and under us, the white angry water, — a picture flashed on us in a second and indelibly impressed on the memory; a picture which I keep to this day, and shall keep till the gallery in which it hangs, with a thousand other perfect ones, crumbles to the foundations.

"The history of bridges is the history of civilization," remarked the Judge. "Waiter, this steak is a trifle underdone. Tell the cook to give it a brief turn on the iron. The cooking is excellent on this line," he remarked, evidently forgetting what he was going to say about bridges, " but it is not up to the level of the Hoffman or of Young's; not quite up," he continued, as if he would, with fine judicial sense, discriminate to a nicety between degrees of excellence in a matter of such supreme importance.

" One would not expect, Judge," I remarked, " to find so old a traveller as yourself so particular touching the cooking of a fillet."

" There is where you mistake," responded the Judge. " He who travels should be an epicure, for his taste must be cosmopolitan. He becomes acquainted with the fruits and vegetables of every zone, the fish of all seas, and the meats of every country. He acquires knowledge not only of the habits but of the beverages of all peoples, and of the *cuisine* of each nation. The knowledge of what he should have causes him to insist on his rights, and the cook who sends me an underdone steak wrongs me as wofully as a government which should suppress the *habeas corpus*. The equities of the stomach should not be trifled with, sir."

" But what about the bridges?" I inquired laughingly, " for I must confess I am more interested in your ideas touching bridges than I am touching steaks."

" I am not responsible for your obtuseness in nondiscrimination between relative values. But bridges are a hobby with me," retorted the Judge. " I studied civil engineering before I did law, and at that time the great bridges of the world had not been built. I can remember when Stephenson laid the foundation of his fame with his first bridge, and the poetry of his great endeavors impressed me profoundly. For a bridge, sir, is a poem put into structure, — an imagination of the mind materialized. It stands for an idea, the idea of human brotherhood and the necessity of friendly exchanges, — that the man on the one side of the river

cannot get along without help from the man on the other side."

"Who built the first bridge, Judge?" inquired the Man from New Hampshire. "Who built the first bridge?"

"It was n't built," replied the Judge; "it was a gift of nature in the form of a tree, which the winds overturned, so that it stretched its trunk of solid wood from bank to bank of the stream, or from edge to edge of the chasm, — a bridge for the panther and bear as well as for the hunter, over the buttresses of which leaves waved, and vines twined their foliage, and under which the torrent thundered and whirled. Man never built a bridge so lovely to look upon as those I have seen in the woods, wind-blown to their places, — the wind-blown bridge of the forest."

"Bravo! bravo!" I exclaimed, and I fluttered the napkin gallantly. "Bravo, Judge! The poetry of the theme has found its poet." And I passed him a section of a delicious French omelet.

"A reminiscence of Paris," remarked the Judge, smiling as he received it.

"More substantial than the pleasures of memory," added the New Hampshire man quietly; and he told the waiter to duplicate the Judge's order.

"There is a characteristic among you New Hampshire men that I admire," remarked the Judge. "You know a good thing when you see it, and you see it mighty quick."

"I see an omelet mighty quick when it's as good as yours," was the retort.

"The gentlemen are out of order," I exclaimed, rapping on the table. "The question before the house is one of bridges."

"Bridge number two," said the Judge, "is that of the settler: two ropes, often woven from roots, with wooden slats intermediate. Then comes the bridge with wooden stringers, planked for heavier travel; then the long enclosed bridge. Mounting still higher in the rising scale is Stephenson's great work, the Victoria Bridge, old style now, but nevertheless a great achievement in engineering, with its monstrous abutments and its thirty acres of painted surface. Rising still higher, we come to the Suspension Bridge at Niagara, and the magnificent cantilever structure of this

road on which we are riding, at Lachine; and crowning all, the great Brooklyn Bridge, over which half a million human beings pass each day. I tell you, gentlemen," exclaimed the Judge earnestly, "the history of bridge-building, from that wind-blown tree-trunk in the woods to the latest achievement in engineering skill, is the history of the human race not only in material progress, but in the apprehension of man's need of his fellow-man and the brotherhood of the race. Every achievement of man is communal. Every embellishment in this car makes companionship more entertaining, and draws us closer together by the bond of common refinement." And the Judge proceeded to call our attention, with critical appreciation, to the carved, the bronzed, and the enamelled elegance of the car.

"That picture reminds me," said the New Hampshire man, pointing to one of the embellishments, a beautiful bit of Japanese enamelling, — "of a little bit of personal experience."

"Waiter," said the Judge, "bring us another pot of coffee and a jug of cream. Thank heaven," he ejaculated, "that I have lived to see the day when one railroad management is so intelligent as to recognize the fact that a man who is rich enough to pay ten dollars a day to travel in a palace car is accustomed to have real cream in his coffee. Now, Colonel," he continued, after he had poured the rich cream slowly in his cup and as slowly poured the hot fragrant coffee upon it, "I am ready for your story. I hope it will have the flavor of true humor in it as this coffee has the flavor of real Java," and he sipped the delicious beverage with the delicacy of one gifted to enjoy the good things of this world.

"Oh, it isn't much of a story," replied the Colonel pleasantly, — "merely a little incident." And he filled his own cup contentedly. "It was in 1868, or thereabouts," quietly continued the Colonel, "when the Orient began to pour the treasures of her art productions, via New Jersey, into Boston, where alone the culture to discriminate between the false and the true in art is to be found, you know, that I was suddenly seized, as were many others, with the 'Japanese craze.' It was a pretty bad attack," he continued reflectively,

CARIBOU ROAD BRIDGE, FRASER.

—" a pretty bad attack. The papers were full of it. Everybody was talking and writing about Japanese art. Now when I buy anything I want it to be first-class, something to be proud of, and feeling mistrustful of my own knowledge, I went to one of the leaders in Boston art circles, and begged him to give me the benefit of his educated taste. He kindly consented to do so, and advised me to allow him to purchase a Japanese screen, as that would be a very beautiful and attractive addition to the furniture of my parlor.

I gave him the money which he said would be needed to purchase a first-class article. It was a pretty steep sum for a screen, I thought, but I knew I could not expect to get a real gem without paying for it. Well, the gentleman, after several days of labor exclusively devoted, as he assured me, to visiting the various 'Eastern Bazaars,' during which he exhausted the focalizing power of several eyeglasses, succeeded in finding what he was after, a real, genuine, first-class specimen of Japanese art, and the huge screen was sent down to my office. It was certainly a wonderful creation. There was a large-sized Durham cow in the centre of the screen, with an almond-eyed milkmaid, in a very low-necked dress and high-heeled French shoes, milking her. The right eye of the cow was fixed intently on the right-hand corner of the screen, while the left glared straight at you. One eye was considerably larger than the other, and of a different color. I naturally concluded that this was a characteristic of Japanese cows, and mentally made a note of it for use if I should ever be called upon to discuss the peculiarities of Oriental art. I made a memorandum also of the fact that there was only half of the cow's tail in the picture, but as the artist had forgotten to paint in a fly for her to practice at, that did not much matter. To the front and at the left of the cow sat a Gordon setter, about half the size of the cow and twice as tall as the girl. The picture affected me so strongly that after I studied it closely, got a photograph of it on my mind, as it were, I quietly shipped it up to my farm in New Hampshire, where I felt there would be room enough for it, and it could add some warmth to the landscape. I hoped also that among my old country neighbors who had never studied high art in Boston it would find plenty of admirers, be a kind of surprise, so to speak. This would have been all right and safe enough if my housekeeper had been a woman of sense and had acted with any judgment; but while cleaning the house one day, she thoughtlessly set the screen out on the lawn, and a series of terrible results followed. In the first place, a herd of cows that a neighbor was

AT BREAKFAST. 41

innocently driving along the street caught a glimpse of the cow on the screen and stampeded. The harmless old man was knocked down and seriously injured, while the cows never stopped running until they got into the next township, where they were impounded as vagrants, and that led to a lawsuit which lasted two or three years and impoverished several families. Next a favorite dog of mine, while chasing a rabbit up the road, saw the Gordon setter on the screen, and dropped dead in his tracks. Then a good, honest, faithful girl who did the milking for the family went out and studied the milkmaid on the screen for several minutes, and going back into the house, promptly applied for her wages "—

"That will do, Colonel," interrupted the Judge, rising, "that will do for your first one." And we all started for the smoking-room.

CHAPTER III.

A VERY HOPEFUL MAN.

<small>Hope springs eternal in the human breast.</small>

HE ancients dreamed of monstrous beings, possessed of monstrous power. The Christian Scriptures tell of a time when there were giants on the earth, and the sons of God married the daughters of men, namely, of a time when the supernal forces were in alliance with the natural, and the hidden energies of the upper reinforced those of the lower sphere. Mythology is full of the same lofty imaginings. Creatures of gigantic size are projected upon her canvas: Cyclops, vast,

abnormal in strength, one-eyed like the headlight of our engine. Had the man who invented the Cyclops invented an engine also, I wonder? Certainly, an old-fashioned Cyclops would seem no more grotesque or appalling to modern scholars than a Mogul engine to a native on the banks of the Ambesi or the shores of the Nyanza. Then there was Vulcan, that mighty armorer for the gods; and Atlas, on whose broad shoulders rested the world; and Minerva, flashing courier of the Empyrean; and later on came Thor with his hammer, pulverizer of mountains, and the whole body of folk-lore threaded through and through with the puissance of dwarf and gnome, of fairy and sprite. All these and other fashionings of the human mind, purely fanciful or semi-real, have come down to us from that murmuring past of which nothing remains save its murmurings, all suggestive of measureless energies, gigantic forms, and mighty forces. The old-time world at least dreamed of almost infinite power and the works of it, in connection with human forms, or forms suggested by the human."

Something like this was said by a scholarly-looking man, who stood with the rest of us on the platform of the rear car of the train, as it whirled round the cliff which brought us in sight of the blue waters of Lake Superior, as they sparkled and flashed brightly under the light of the morning. He who has rolled for fifty miles along the shore of this majestic body of inland water, who has seen the summer sky arching the blue dome above it, its forest-covered islands, the hundreds of islets that dot its surface, its curving beaches of brown and yellow sand, its deep, secluded bays and rocky promontories, has looked upon one of the most entertaining and charming pictures of the continent, — a picture which delights the beholder as he gazes, and remains fixed, with all its changeful colors, in his memory ever after.

"What the ancients dreamed," remarked the Judge, referring to what the scholarly-looking man had said, "we moderns see realized. Our telegraph is swifter than Minerva; and that common laborer, who is guarding that bridge yonder, can for a shilling send a message faster than they ever dreamed Jupiter could do it. Atlas is no longer a myth. We to-day know the power that holds up the world: it is the same that keeps this car on the track — gravitation. Cyclops is no longer a terror. He is ahead of us, and our engineer has him in perfect control. Thor is our servant, and he pulverizes mountains at so much a cubic foot; while the gnome that bored its way through this spur of quartz, tunnelling it for our passage, is the diamond drill." And as the Judge concluded the sentence, we all retired into the car, to escape the smoke and the cinders.

"It seems to me," continued the scholarly-looking man, after we were seated, "that the thinkers of the world get more credit than they should, as compared with the doers. My life has been spent in the pursuit of letters," he continued, "and my thoughts have been favored with a kindly reception by the world; my writings have brought me both money and fame. But as I have seen the excavations along this line; as I

BLACKFEET ENCAMPMENT

have been rolled over its bridges, and noted that the fairy-like iron structure beneath me gave no tremor; as I have seen that the solid sides of cliffs had been cut out for our path as if they were made of chalk, I have felt that the words, and even the thoughts, of men, however eloquently expressed, were as nothing when compared with their deeds. I know not who built this road, whose imagination audaciously conceived it, or whose courage constructed it; but whoever did do it has in it erected an imperishable monument."

"It is indeed a magnificent result," said a gentleman, an old, gray-headed engineer from Nebraska, who surveyed the route for the Union Pacific, and made for himself a name in that and other trans-continental enterprises, — "a magnificent work indeed." And he gazed thoughtfully through the open door at the level road-bed and gleaming rails. "It cost not only millions of money, but human lives as well," he continued. "On this very section, within a space of twenty miles, over two millions of dollars' worth of dynamite was used, and some men, I am told, were wounded or blown to pieces."

"Dreadful!" exclaimed the scholarly-looking man. "What more horrible death could a man die?"

"I do not regard death by dynamite as the worst of accidents," said a voice.

"The devil!" exclaimed the Judge. "What's that, sir?" and every eye in the compartment was suddenly fixed upon the man.

He was not a large man, he was even a small one,

and there was nothing fierce or reckless in his appearance, nor would one pick him out as a man specially endowed with courage, or even gifted with extraordinary persistence. He was not a man of full habit, but spare in flesh. His complexion was sallow and leathery. He had large gray eyes, weakly prominent, and

somewhat faded. His hair was thin, not positive in color, and his neck had but little base to it. Not one of us had even noticed him before. Indeed, we might have ridden with him for days, and not one of us would have noticed him, had he not given utterance to such a horrible sentiment, an expression which sounded all the more horrible because of the mildness of the tone which accompanied it.

"I said," repeated the little man, looking benevolently at the Judge, — "I said I did not regard death by dynamite as the worst of accidents."

The Judge glared at the little man for a moment through his eyeglasses. He removed the glasses from his nose, wiped them carefully, and replacing them, took another savage look at the man, who sat quietly in the corner.

"Gad, sir!" he exclaimed, at length. "*I* can't conceive a worse death than being blown to pieces, quick as a flash, without any warning, — think of it, sir, — by dynamite!"

"No doubt," returned the little man, mildly, "such a death is somewhat sudden, and, physically considered, is liable to make a total wreck of a man. The conductor told me a few minutes ago that one of the gentlemen who was dynamited was actually distributed — that's the word, as I recall it, that he used — so much so that there was never anything found of him, only a thumb or some such thing; not enough, it was decided by the authorities, to make a funeral of. Nevertheless, I still respectfully maintain that worse things can happen to a man than death by dynamite."

I will confess that I was never more shocked in my life than at the horrible account which the little man in the corner had given of one of the sad accidents which had occurred during the building of the road, and it was made all the more horrible from his manner of telling it; for he had told the dreadful tale in the calmest and most placid of tones, his mild, large gray eyes fixed calmly on the face of the Judge, and without the least movement whatever of any feature of his face. I think I may safely say that every other gentleman of the party felt in the same way, and that the eyes of all of us were directed upon him in amazement, not to say indignation.

"What could a man meet that would be more dreadful?" exclaimed the Judge, excitedly, and he glared at the inoffensive stranger through his eyeglasses as if he would perforate him.

The stranger never winced under the stare of the Judge. He did not even appear nettled in the least, for his eyes, without a shade of change in their expression, fixed their gaze placidly upon him, level with his own.

"We judge of these things probably from the standpoint of experience," he mildly remarked, "and I have personally experienced many things worse than dynamite."

"We should be pleased, sir, to hear of your experiences," sneeringly remarked the Judge, and his look was one calculated to burst his eyeglasses from their frames.

"It is not worth your attention, gentlemen," he replied pleasantly, bowing. "It is not worth your attention, I am quite sure, for I have in one sense had nothing remarkable happen to me, and I will detain you but a moment, and that because you pleasantly insist upon it," — a hit which must have made the Judge wince. And resuming, he gave us the following vindication of his judgment : —

"I have been shipwrecked, been baked in a railroad accident, and fired out of a foundry window by a boiler explosion. I was shot in the neck at Gettysburg, suffered starvation in Libby Prison, fell overboard from a transport off Charleston, and left four of my fingers in the mouth of a shark. I had my right arm broken in two places in a New York riot, and stood on a barrel with a halter round my neck in a Southern town, at the outbreak of the great Rebellion, from sunrise to sunset. I was buried under the ruins of a building in San Francisco during an earthquake, and dug out after fifty hours of imprisonment. I have been shot at three times, twice by lunatics and once by a highwayman. I was buried two days by a gas explosion in a mine, and narrowly escaped lynching last year in Arizona through mistaken identity. And though I am over fifty, and have nearly lost the use of my right leg; have just had, as I understand, all my property, on which there was no insurance, destroyed by fire in a Western town; and the doctor in New York to whom I went last week for an examination assures me that I will soon be bedridden from rheumatism, nevertheless," he added cheerfully, "while I undoubtedly have met some obstacles in the past, I still refuse to believe that luck is against me."

It was not a question of propriety — none of us thought of that. Had we done so our action might have been different. But at the conclusion of the little man's narration of his experiences, of the history of his life, there went up a roar of laughter that might have lifted the truck from the rails. Indeed, it broke up the party. One after another, we went forward to the main compartment of the car, and took our usual seats. Several of the gentlemen apparently began to read, but I noticed that they held their papers as if they were near-sighted, and that the papers shook till they rattled. The Judge sat directly ahead of me. In one hand he held his eyeglasses, and with the other he wiped his eyes with his handkerchief. At last he turned halfway round in his chair, and bending toward me, while his face was convulsed and the water stood in his eyes, said, —

"Dynamite! Gad! dynamite is n't so bad, after all!"

CHAPTER IV.

THE BIG NEPIGON TROUT.

<blockquote>We may say of angling as Dr. Boteler said of strawberries: "Doubtless God could have made a better berry, but doubtless God never did." And so, if I might judge, God never did make a more calm, quiet, innocent recreation than angling.   ISAAK WALTON.</blockquote>

"CIVILIZATION means luxury," said the Judge sententiously, as he looked complacently over the dinner-table, with its snowy linen, its delicate china, its burnished plate, its cut-glass ware, and its vase of woodland flowers. " It is that fine arrangement by which matter is made to minister to mind, the lower compelled to assist the higher. The provision made for travel is the best measure of American progress."

"Analyze the matter, Judge," I said, as I passed

him the *menu*. "Analyze the matter, and tell us what civilization has to do with you and me at this moment."

"Bouillon," said the Judge to the waiter.

"Mock-turtle," I added.

"Mock-turtle is too heavy for summer," said the Judge peremptorily to me. "Like the majority of Americans, you have lived in spite of yourself. You have the senses of a Greek and the appetite of a barbarian. The man who eats mock-turtle soup in summer is a proof that the principle of divine preservation is still active."

"There's nothing to bouillon," I retorted. "It's only water with a hint of a flavor in it, and the hint is n't always very plain, either."

"That's the beauty of it," returned the Judge. "That's the beauty of it," he exclaimed, as he fixed a dainty *boutonnière* of choice flowers stolen from the vase to the lapel of his coat. "The civilized man abhors grossness. The barbarian feeds at a trough. Educate him, and he erects a table. Knife and fork replace his fingers, and as you refine him the number of his dishes increases, adornments multiply, until at last he is lifted to that level upon which you and I live, where the nose and the eye eat with the mouth, and the furniture of the table, in the elegance of its appointments, magnifies the feast."

By this time, the soup had been brought, and for a moment the conversation ceased. We were running between some lofty hills. Here and there we passed a small clearing, with its little log-house in the centre. Each narrow field was a mass of woodland flowers, scarlet, purple, and white, standing as if planted in separate beds, characterizing the field with color. The cabins here and there were covered with clambering vines, and on their sodden roofs the birds and winds, those planters of the air, had sown the seeds for flowering, fruitful growth. Outside, the world was warm and odorous. The wild-flowers sweetened it, and the wind which blew the scented air through our open windows and into our nostrils brought from the lofty hills wild, gamy scents, and pungencies of fir and pine.

The Judge sipped his bouillon delicately, as if every

drop were a separate ministration to his palate. His eyes contemplated with pleased satisfaction, not only the glorious color of the flowers, the green of the hills, and the blue sky, but also the amber-tinted liquid in his spoon; while his nostrils expanded as if they would inhale more abundantly the perfume that drifted through the window. It was impossible not to see in him the incarnation of refined physical enjoyment, a man who honored his appetite by gratifying it, but who gratified it in a manner so delicate that he not only redeemed it from the least appearance of grossness, but made its gratification the means for the display of his virtues.

"I have travelled," remarked the Judge reflectively, "in most of the countries of the world. I have suffered in the tropics from heat, and in the Arctic regions from cold. For the sake of seeing a few old ruins, mostly buried in sand, I have borne the agony of prolonged thirst on the Desert, and that I might go a little farther than some one else up some river or over some mountain, I have inflicted upon my body the pangs which precede starvation. But I have come to that period of life in which man ceases to be an impulsive, and becomes a reasoning, animal. And while the spirit of the tourist is in me as strongly as ever, I nevertheless insist that, in return for my money, civilization shall give me, as I journey, three things: safety, comfort, luxury. If it will give me these, — and I assure you thousands feel as I do upon the subject, — I will give my money, and go and see what it has that is new to show me. If not, I will stay at home."

FRASER CAÑON, ABOVE SPUZZUM

I must confess that I was impressed with the conclusion that the Judge had reached, the more so, perhaps, because it was the first time I had ever heard it so clearly formulated; and I presume my face manifested the interest which I felt in his line of remark, for after he had tasted of each of the vegetables before him, as a lady might examine several samples of lace, and deftly prepared the fish for its dressing, he resumed: —

"I am an illustration of my theory, sir. I have crossed the continent twenty times, I presume. I have traveled on every other line repeatedly, but I had never seen the prairie lands west of Winnipeg, which an old friend who came over this route last summer wrote me 'were as beautiful as the valley of the Platte, and as lovely as the Laramie plains — the most beautiful stretch of prairie land in the world,' he said. And from the Black Cañon of the Fraser River he wrote me eight pages describing it. He is nearly seventy years old, bear in mind; — eight pages of description — an old forty-niner at that — that was simply wild, sir, wild and extravagant as the description of a boy; and it is because of those letters from my old friend concerning these Canadian prairies we shall see to-morrow, and the four hundred miles of mountain scenery lying west of the prairies, that I undertook the journey. But, sir," he added, with emphasis, "I would never have undertaken it unless I had ascertained that I could travel with safety and with comfort, and be provided, as I journeyed, with certain luxuries."

"Nevertheless, Judge," I remarked, "the loveliness and majesties of nature are a compensation for occasional deprivations, are they not?"

"Within certain limitations, I should agree with you," he replied. "But for myself, the amber of my bouillon assists me to appreciate more perfectly the flowers blooming in that little clearing. The taste of this salmon in my mouth makes that stretch of water yonder seem more charming; and I am confident that the ice-cream, the nuts, and the coffee which I see are provided for our dessert will give to the sky a bluer tint, and add softness to the fleece of yonder clouds."

Thus the conversation flowed on, while the train glided along past the beaches of the bays that set deeply into the mountains which characterize, with their massive formations, the northern shore of Lake Superior. The Judge was in his best mood, and talked as only one who has seen much of the world, its peoples, and its ways can talk. Each course was duly honored, as if it were the only one to be enjoyed, and the "table hour," as the Judge, with a pleasant conceit, named it, was the one so utilized that while it ministered most fully to the wants of the body, it contributed beyond any other to the pleasures of the mind.

"Hello!" I exclaimed, as I glanced at the time-table, which, in the form of an illustrated itinerary, lay on the table. "We must be nearing the Nepigon."

"The Nepigon!" exclaimed the Judge, with the ardor of a sportsman. "More monstrous trout have been caught in the Nepigon than in any other river on the continent. I have friends who firmly believe that it is one of the four sacred rivers that flowed out of Paradise."

"I think I would agree with them," I laughingly

returned, "if they would make their Paradise include not only the river, but the lake in which it heads. For if Lake Nepigon was not in Paradise, it was a great loss for Paradise." And as I spoke, the train struck the bridge which stretches across the noble and noted river, and as it was gliding smoothly on it slowed, and suddenly stopped.

"Oh! oh! oh!"

"See, Tom! Look!"

"Jones, where are you?"

"Fo' de Lawd, Mars' Judge!" exclaimed the waiter. "You two gem'men git to de hind end ob de kyar, ef you wants ter see what's gwine on down dar in dat ribber!"

The excitement was contagious, for the car was full of shouts, cheers, and exclamations. The Judge rushed down the aisle to the rear of the car —

"Great heavens!" he exclaimed, as he reached the platform. "Look at that!"

A hundred feet below us flowed the noble current, a deep, wide, strong-moving mass of water. Here and there an eddy marked it with its huge circumference. But in the main it moved downward toward the great lake, shining in full view, as a river flows between widened banks and with plenty of room. In the middle of the river nearly under us was a canoe with an Indian at either end, and a man in a velveteen jacket standing in the centre. In his hands was a rod, and the tip of the rod was doubled backward nigh to the reel, the ringing whir of which filled the air. His pose was that of an angler who had struck a fish — a big fish, a fish that is fighting him gamely and stubbornly, and which he is resisting with the cool, determined skill of a veteran of the rod.

"What a picture!" exclaimed the Judge. "Gad! what a picture!"

Well might he exclaim, "What a picture!" The wide river; the island-studded lake, into which it emptied; the lofty banks; the great dome of blue sky above; high over the stream, as if hung in mid-air, the long train, every window filled with heads, every platform crowded with forms, the engineer, an angler himself, hanging out of the cab, swinging his hat; below, the canoe, the ochred Indians, the bent body of the angler, the swaying, quivering, doubled-up rod, — what a picture!

Suddenly, we who were looking saw the rod straighten. Some of us knew what it meant. The Judge clinched my arm, and in an instant out of the water came the trout, mouth open, fins extended, tail spread.

"Jerusalem!" screamed the Judge. "He's a twenty-pounder!"

Dear old Judge, thou hadst the true angler's eye — that eye which enlarges and multiplies by a happy trick of vision, not merely the size of the fish, but the enjoyment of the soul. Ay, ay, it was a twenty-pounder to both of us old sports for the instant, and if the envious scales did shrink the noble form to shorter and thinner proportions, it could not rob us of the ecstasy of our first estimate, thank heaven!

And the fight that followed — what words may set

"JERUSALEM! HE'S A TWENTY-POUNDER!"

it forth? O anglers, shut your eyes, and see and hear it from behind your closed lids. Call memory to your aid — the memory of the sternest fight you ever fought, of the swiftest torrent, of the wildest pool, of that favorite rod smashed to splinters, of paddle broken, of the "biggest fish that ever swam" lost or won. Stop, I say, and from behind closed lids see all this, and you will see what we saw under the great bridge over the Nepigon on that bright June day.

Whoever the Man in the Velveteen Jacket might be, he was of the right sort, an angler of whom anglers need never be ashamed; for as he fought that fish he gave us such an exhibition of angler's fence as ranked him one of the best that ever fingered reel. An eight-ounce rod against an eight-pound fish, a strong, deep current, and a Nepigon canoe: grant anglers such conditions, and how many shall make a winning fight?

Twice the huge fish broke water, and twice the long train cheered him to the echo. The Judge was wild. Each time the fish broke the surface, he fairly jumped. He leaned far over the rail. He swung his hat, and when the monstrous trout broke the surface the second time, he yelled, —

"Save him, save him, and I'll nominate you for the Presidency!"

Once the great fish for an instant burst through his opponent's guard. Once I must confess my heart sank within me, as a stone sinks to the bottom of a well. When he was a hundred feet from the canoe, the rod nearly tip and butt, and the silk line stretched through the air like a wire, the fish doubled and lanced backward like a flash. We saw his wake, — that sharpened wedge of water which anglers dread, — and as he went under the canoe, and in the stillness that had come to us we heard the line rattle on the bark, a groan escaped the Judge. He rolled his eyes upward, and roared as if stricken with pain, —

"Great Scott! he 's lost him!"

But the fish was not lost. The angler recovered his advantage, and fought the fight to the end, skilfully and coolly. The fish was deftly gaffed by one of the Indians, and quickly lay on the bottom of the canoe. The Indians seized their paddles, and the light craft glanced toward the western bank, the man unjointing his rod as the boat shot along, and in a moment they came panting up the embankment with a huge hamper in their hands, in which, amid flowers and grasses, lay six other trout, nearly as large as the one we had seen captured.

Seldom is such a reception granted to a mortal as was given to the Man in the Velveteen Jacket. The engineer cheered and swung his hat; the fireman, sooted and begrimed, capered and danced on the coal-box like an electrified imp; the passengers yelled; the ladies fluttered their handkerchiefs; while we anglers of the party fairly took him in our arms and lifted him on to the platform, where the Judge enfolded him in an embrace which the stranger will never forget, — a hug such as an old angler gives a younger one to whom he is indebted for an exhibition of skill which has brought back to his memory all his own former victories, and proved to his anxious soul that the gentle art is not being neglected.

Never fear, never fear, dear old Judge, that the art of all arts will be lost, or the skill of trained finger and eye be forgotten. We shall pass; but still the streams will flow on, the pools will go round, and the trout love the coolness of springs and the rush of swift waters. The boys will grow up like their sires, loving water and sun, loving forest and rapids. With brown faces and hands, and with eyes keen as ours, they will stand where we stood, they will boat where we boated, they will camp where we camped, and the dead ashes of fires that we kindled they will kindle to new life again. The gentle art will live on, while nature is nature and mankind is man.

CHAPTER V.

THE MAN IN THE VELVETEEN JACKET.

A merrier man
Within the limit of becoming mirth
I never spent an hour's talk withal.

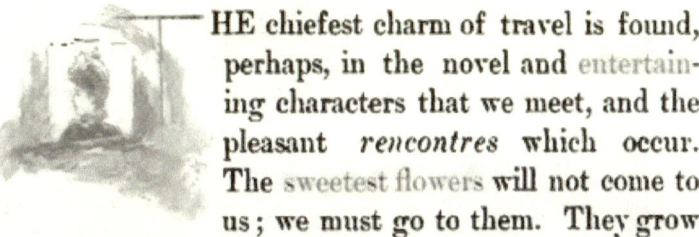THE chiefest charm of travel is found, perhaps, in the novel and entertaining characters that we meet, and the pleasant *rencontres* which occur. The sweetest flowers will not come to us; we must go to them. They grow in the nooks and corners of fences, in cracks and crannies of the rocks, in crevices of the cliffs, in strange out-of-the-way places, where only the eye and the nose of the trailer may find them. In respect to human companionship it is the same; the quaint, the intelligent, the charming, the original and piquant personalities of the race are not born in groups; they are not

found in clusters, nor can we call them to our homes. To find them we must travel; we must look them up; we must go where they are; we must put ourselves upon currents which cross their currents, and so, like birds flying at random, be blown together.

The finest delight of travel is that of the casual companionships it brings us, the smiles and the bright faces that we see, the kindly hands that we clasp, or the warm hearts that we meet in our need. These make the charm of journeying, and cause the recollections of voyaging to be so delightful.

And this man — this Man in the Velveteen Jacket — was such a gift to our party. It is true, he had come to us recommended as no other man might be. His introduction accredited him to our fellowship as the word of a king might not do, and from the moment he entered our circle it was as one who belonged there, as one who filled a place that had waited for him and remained unfilled until he came; and into it he dropped without undue familiarity, on the one hand, and without the least awkwardness or embarrassment, on the other.

His manners were simply charming, because of a happy mingling of modesty and self-possession. He was a natural humorist. His humor was so quaint that it amused, and so gravely expressed that it puzzled. As you looked at his face and listened to the tones of his voice, you were divided in feeling as to whether you were listening to fiction or to fact; and even amid your laughter at the ludicrousness of the creation, you found yourself querying whether the source of the fun at which you were laughing was not found in some serious occurrence.

"You did it well," said the Judge, referring to his contest with the trout. "You never made a miss with eye or finger. You handled the rod as only a man can who has handled it from boyhood."

The Man in the Velveteen Jacket looked at the Judge for a moment, with the most mirthful of lights in his eyes, as one who found in his positive assertion a suggestion of fun, which all of us appreciated at the Judge's expense when he remarked, —

"I am happy to think that my manner of fighting the fish met the approbation of an old angler like yourself, but as measured by time I would scarcely be regarded as an expert, for I never touched a rod till I was twenty-five."

"Incredible!" exclaimed the Judge. "Why, sir, I have always maintained that no man could become an expert with the rod unless he began practice with it as a boy, — grew up with it, as it were."

"Nevertheless," continued the stranger pleasantly, "the fact is as I have stated it. Until I was twenty-five I used the gun. Shooting was a passion with me. It was my favorite pastime, and I presume I should never have used the rod at all — which I have done exclusively since a certain event — unless I had met with a great misfortune, caused by a dog, — a misfortune which made me lose all taste for shooting and the sight of a bird dog absolutely disagreeable to me. Yes, gentlemen," continued the Man in the Velveteen Jacket, earnestly, "my last experience with a dog was

MT. CARROLL, FROM THE WEST.

a most unfortunate one, and although years have elapsed since I met it, I cannot recall it, even at this distance of time, without an involuntary shudder. Strange that a man's life can be seriously affected by what seems at the start a trivial event! But I assure you that my profession, the location of my residence, and my domestic connection, are all to-day different from what they would have been had I never met that dog."

It is needless to say that the astonishing statement of our companion excited our curiosity to a degree, and our looks doubtless plainly apprised him of the fact; for after a moment's pause, he took his pipe from his mouth, and having emptied the ashes into the cuspidor as carefully as if he were smoking in a friend's parlor, with his friend's wife sitting in the next room, in exact range of the door which commanded his position, he continued, —

"Perhaps it is only fair that I should satisfy your curiosity, which I see I have awakened by what may seem to you an extraordinary statement; and if it will entertain you to hear a story which has little to recommend it save its novelty and its sadness, I will, at the cost of painful reminiscence, tell it to you."

Upon this the Judge, who, because of the dignity of his official position as well as of his years, and, I may add, the urbanity of his manners, was by mutual assent of us all regarded as the natural spokesman of the party, replied, —

"I must confess that I am curious to hear the history of the dog, or of your experiences with the dog;

and I doubt not that all the gentlemen here share this sentiment with me; and if your feelings will allow you to satisfy our curiosity, I beg you to do so. For it does seem extraordinary that a dog should be able to influence a man's life to such an extent as to change the direction of his activities, and even affect his domestic environment."

"You must know, then, gentlemen," resumed the man, "that I studied for the practice of medicine, and was engaged to the daughter of a noted physician, who lived in the northern section of Vermont and enjoyed a large and lucrative country practice. He was a man of large attainments and of a high spirit. His only daughter was a young lady of unusual beauty, and had been endowed at birth with a liberal share of her father's abilities and his excitable temperament. She was a lovely girl, and, being sole heiress prospectively to the old doctor's property, was much courted by her gentlemen acquaintances. When, therefore, our engagement became known I was, with good reason, heartily congratulated by the generous, and cordially hated by the envious. I had just been graduated at the medical school, and at the close of my summer vacation it was arranged that the lady and myself should be married. This would enable me to begin my practice under her father, the old doctor, whose business would thus naturally, in the course of time, fall into my hands. I submit, gentlemen, if any young man ever stood face to face with a more auspicious future. I was soon to be united to a beautiful girl, with an ample fortune, and be thereby admitted to a professional connection which was both gratifying to my vanity and satisfactory to my ambition. And even now, after years have passed, I cannot recall without emotion that I lost wife and fortune, and that a most beautiful arrangement of Providence was disturbed, broken up, smashed, so to speak, by a miserable dog."

By this time, as can well be imagined, we were all of us intensely interested in the gentleman's narrative. We felt that his had been no common experience, but that in the life of the Man in the Velveteen Jacket there was embodied a series of startling mishaps, and that, however he might strive to disguise it by forced calmness of voice or restraint of feature, we were nevertheless about to listen to the recital of a lifelong bereavement — perhaps of a tragedy. We therefore drew our circle the more closely around him, that we might not lose a single word that came from his lips. And I could see that the Judge, who was endowed with acute sensibilities, had prophetically sensed what was coming, for his eyes glistened appreciatively behind his glasses, and his large checked silk handkerchief was spread carefully over his plump knees, ready to his hand.

"It all happened in this way," he continued, after a moment's silence, devoted doubtless by him to sad recollections. "It all happened in this way. A few days after Commencement, when I had everything packed, and was ready to go to the doctor's to make the preliminary arrangements for the wedding, a club of fellow-sportsmen invited me to dinner. I had, of course, a most enjoyable evening. I believe there was not a man at the table over whose dog I had not shot;

and between the speeches, the songs, the anecdotes, and the reminiscences of flood and field, our mirthfulness was unbounded. All knew of the good fortune ahead of me, and each and every one, I verily believe, heartily rejoiced at it. Amid all the changes of life," said the Man in the Velveteen Jacket reflectively, " amid all the changes of life, and the passage of years which have obliterated much, I have never forgotten that happy evening, or the features of a single face around those tables."

"Amen!" exclaimed the Judge, who was himself a noted sportsman. "Amen to the noble sentiment. There is no comradeship like that of the woods and waters, no friendship like that of out-door men." And the old sportsman's eulogy was greeted by the applause of us all.

"The next morning I was at my bank, getting a check cashed, *en route* for the depot, and being pressed for time, was getting hurriedly into a coupé at the door, when two friends — a committee appointed by the club — rushed up to the carriage, having a large pointer dog and a speech to deliver to me. I hastily explained my position to them : that I had n't a minute to spare, and that I must reach the train ; that the coupé was full of parcels and baskets ; that I was truly grateful, but I did not see how I could make room —

"I am not sure that my friends heard me clearly, for there was a great noise in the street, and the driver, who knew that there was n't an instant to lose, had started his horse. Be that as it may, the dog was delivered to me. For, unfortunately, the window of the coupé was open, and my two friends, seizing the dog in their hands, pushed him with great merriment through the aperture, throwing a huge parchment pedigree into my lap at the same time.

"As might be expected, the dog was considerably distributed when he landed in the carriage. One muddy forefoot went in between my shirt-front and white vest, and the other lanced along the back side of my neck. His right hind foot was buried in a basket of grapes, and his left had ploughed through a huge and costly bouquet of flowers, bursting the band which held them together. Still, I reflected that the dog wasn't to blame for being so unceremoniously thrust through a window, and the motive on the part of my friends which prompted the gift was touching. So I collected the different parts of the dog as much as I could, brought him to one centre, as it were, and pressing him down between my legs, tied him by a neck-rope to a big telescope valise on the seat beside me.

"I had just got the dog safely fixed in this manner, and was collecting the scattered flowers, when the coupé thundered up to the depot. The Jehu jumped from his box and threw open the door, crying, 'Hurry up, zur, not a minit to spare.'

"I grabbed the basket of grapes in one hand, my hat-box in the other, and jumped to the pavement. But the dog was as anxious to get out as I was. For as I was making my exit he bolted between my legs, my big valise was yanked from the seat, and striking me between the shoulders, knocked me on top of the dog. Thinking I had done it on purpose, he whipped his tail between his legs and rushed into the depot, yelling at every jump, with the valise thumping along after him, while I plunged for it in order to recapture the dog.

"Now there happened to be a big, corpulent hackman carrying a huge trunk on his shoulders across the platform, and my dog, like an infernal idiot, fetched a circle clean round his legs, and then started to jump the track. The man's feet were jerked from under him, the big trunk dropped heavily to the platform and burst open, and my valise flew around and hit him in the stomach as he sat down; while the dog, who had begun to feel that he was being unjustly treated, doubled back and charged at the big hackman with bared teeth and tail stiff as a ramrod. I never saw a madder man or a worse muss in my life. The hackman addressed me in language which was simply frightful, and I was inexpressibly grateful when, with the help of a brakeman, I succeeded in getting that dreadful dog into the baggage-car and saw him lashed safely to a stanchion. The flowers were lost, the basket of grapes was left behind, my clothes were tracked all over as if I had served as a mat to a dog-kennel, and my poor valise looked as tired as a compositor at four o'clock in the morning.

"I got an express tag and wrote my name on it, and where I was going, gave the dog some water and the baggage-master two dollars to put him off carefully at the station where I was to stop, and then I went back

THE HACKMAN.

to the parlor car and spent an hour with the porter in getting the dog tracks off my wardrobe.

"Well, along in the afternoon, when we had got well up into Vermont, the train stopped at a small station for wood and water, and I strolled forward to see if my dog was all right and make his acquaintance a little. To my horror, I discovered that a new baggage-man had come aboard, and reading the directions wrongly, had put my dog off at a village nearly fifty miles back in New Hampshire. There was only one thing to do, and that was to go back after him. Fortunately the down train was due in a few moments, and when it came in I boarded it. I reached the town about seven in the evening, and not a bit too soon, for my dog had already made a record for himself, and was acting in a manner to secure an obituary notice of at least a column in length in the next issue of the village paper. The station-master had received him from the baggage-man, and not knowing to whom he should deliver him, had very properly tied him to a trunk in the baggage-room, locked him in, and gone home. In two or three hours he became tired of waiting, and gnawing his rope in two went out through the window, taking half the sash with him. No sooner had he touched the ground than the station-master's dog pitched upon him, and after a short experience he started up the principal street of the village, as near the centre as a dog in a hurry could estimate with my dog in exact line and only one jump behind him. The two had gone into the station-agent's house, as near the same instant as they could have done if they had practiced a hundred years. The man was at supper with his family, in the act of saying grace, and when the two dogs went under the table they lifted it as much as three feet straight up in the air. The agent's wife went into hysterics, his oldest daughter fainted where she sat, and the man, without waiting to collect his own dog, chased mine into the street with a shot-gun in his hand, yelling 'Mad dog! mad dog!' at the top of his voice. He would undoubtedly have killed my dog, had he not stopped to take aim, and it was owing to this slight mistake, probably, that my dog escaped with his life.

"I never knew how I got out of that town alive, for I insulted every man that spoke to me, and got into two fights while the light lasted. But I did, and had the dog with me, too, for I was pretty hot over the treatment we both had received in that village, and moreover, I hold that every man ought to stand by his dog."

"That's right," said the Judge, as he wiped his eyes. "Yes, every man ought to stand by his dog, in court and out of court."

And for several minutes the Man in the Velveteen Jacket was unable to proceed because of the emotions his story had elicited from those who sat listening to his vivid narration.

"But all this," he resumed at length, — "all this, in itself considered, was of very little importance, nothing more than any man who has had a dog with a pedigree given him might expect to have happen. I would not even have mentioned it were it not that it is necessary you should know these precedent trivialities in order that you may appreciate what follows, and understand how it was that the dog ruined me, and I became an angler.

"I got the dog home at last, and put him into the hospital, for he had been considerably rattled and was out of repairs, so to speak. So I wrote to my fiancée that I was unexpectedly detained from my anticipated visit by a sprained ankle, but that I had the ankle under treatment, and would surely be with her the next week. I also told her that I had been presented with a beautiful pointer dog, one of the liveliest and brightest animals I had ever met, and that I would bring my pet over when I came, and I pleasantly added the following:—

"'P. S. How delightful it is, my darling, that both of us have a pet,— you a favorite cat, I an amiable dog,— with which to begin our married life and enliven our domestic circle.'

"Alas! how little," exclaimed the Man in the Velveteen Jacket plaintively, — "how little can we mortals anticipate what is ahead of us!

"The dog was one of those irrepressible specimens of canine exuberance that you could but admire," he continued. "He was a born hunter, if there ever was one. He was nobly free from partiality, and hunted one class of objects as readily as another. All scents in his nose meant game. An old hen was a delight to his soul, and a calf kept his spirits from depression. A stray pig was a godsend, and a timid, half-broken colt threw him into ecstacies. But if there was one thing on the earth that he yearned for more than another, it was a cat. A large, well-built, positive-minded, masculine cat represented a whole hemisphere of game to him. He was a bird-dog nominally, but practically his pedigree starred him with universal adaptations. Nevertheless, at the sight of a cat he became supersensitive. At that moment there was no hesitation in him. He acted spontaneously and in a straight line. At such an opportunity he was always at full cock and went off himself. Then it was that he seemed possessed of a human soul, and to realize that beautiful moral maxim that 'he who hesitates is lost.'"

"Oh, Lord!" said the Judge, and reaching up to his linen duster he extracted a fresh handkerchief.

It was not because there was any remarkable humor in the story that the Man in the Velveteen Jacket was telling that we were affected so strongly, but because of his happy mannerism in telling it, and the lightness of our own dispositions. For he told it with a quaintness of expression and a lightness of touch that left nothing to be desired by the hearer, and all of us were in a mind to be tickled, and hence we received the reflections of his humor as the water receives the sky, and I have often noted that the humor of the humorist and that of the audience equally contribute to the laughter that ensues. Be this as it may, we all laughed with the abandonment of children at the narrative he was telling. And when he began again he did so with even a quicker movement and a livelier manner of expression. If it were fiction he was narrating, he had evidently begun to enjoy it as if it were real; and if it were fact, the original sadness of the event was now wholly obliterated by the mirthfulness of the recollection.

"A happier man than I never breathed the morning air," he resumed, "when I started across the country to visit the home of my betrothed. I pictured to myself, as I swung along the country road, the joy of our meeting and the happiness of our future lives. I knew that the old doctor had a temper like a Turk, and that my beloved was impulsive. But I reflected with satisfaction that the one could not in the order of nature live forever, and that the earnest temperament of the other would doubtless be mollified by the softening influence of my example.

"My dog, to which I had already become attached, shared the buoyancy of my spirits. He fastened himself joyfully on to every calf that he met, and abbreviated the tail of every chicken he encountered. The whole country grew profane in his wake, and I knew that every shot-gun was being loaded for his return. Happy in the excitement he created, he distributed his favors on either side of the road with ingenuous impartiality, and hunted with equal zest the pigs in the meadows and the cats in the porches. The dogs that limped into their kennels after he had passed were dazed with the quickness of their experience, and I doubt not that the religious element of that section remembers to this day his advent as a visitation.

"I shall never be able, gentlemen, to make you understand what happened. Even to me, after years of reflection, it remains a nightmare of wild sights and savage sounds; a kaleidoscopic mixture of colors and forms; a vision of a dreadful meeting and a more awful parting,—a meeting and a parting which, from the circumstances of the case, could never be repeated.

"With fond anticipations I turned a corner in the road and suddenly stood within a few rods of the house; and there, gentlemen, oh, there was my fiancée waving her handkerchief to me, while the old doctor, seated in his gig, was proudly showing off the paces of a half-broken four-year-old colt he had recently purchased. Impelled by feelings too strong to be restrained, I swung my hat joyfully over my head, gave a cheerful halloo, and rushed forward. That infernal idiot of a dog, hearing my cry, seeing me swinging my hat and rushing down the road, went for that prancing colt like a freckled meteor. The colt saw him coming and gave a tremendous bound, and as the dog went under him in a cloud of dust, he opened two holes as big as a hat through the dashboard of the gig, and then bolted down the road.

"Never did I see a horse and a dog lay themselves lower down to the ground. Each was running from a motive, and each had an object in view. Under such favorable conditions their pace was terrific and both attended strictly to business. The old doctor was standing up in the gig, his stubbly gray hair pointing toward the home he was leaving, pulling like a windlass at the reins, his linen duster flying behind him, and a stream of small bottles pouring out of each pocket!

THE RUNAWAY COLT

"I stood hat in hand aghast at the sight, but — I swear to you, gentlemen, had I died for it the next minute, I could not have helped it — laughing until the tears stood in my eyes. Suddenly I looked at my betrothed, and then I nearly dropped. I saw by the look in her face that it was all up with me, that my world had stopped, and that the sun would nevermore rise on the hills of my love.

"*She thought I had set that miserable dog on the colt!*

"She never opened her mouth, but silently went into the house. I followed. I spoke as a man naturally would in such circumstances. There was no haughtiness in my voice. She simply turned and looked at me. Gentlemen, there was no love in her eyes, not a trace! Then she said, —

"'Sir!!!'

"Still I fought for my life. Wife and fortune were trembling in the balance. I saw it. I pleaded. I knelt, — yes, I knelt at her feet; I poured out my vows; I seized her unwilling hand; I saw I was making headway. She began to relent. There was a chance, a fighting chance, as it were. My heart bounded with hope. Gentlemen, I should have won, — I give you my word, I should have won. By a close calculation of chances, you can see I should have won. When, — suddenly I heard a sound, — a sound I recognized, and glancing toward the door, there! — there stood that damnable dog! And that was n't the worst of it, he was looking at something! looking steadily and fixedly at something, with that coppery and unearthly look in his eyes I had grown to know so well. Involuntarily I followed the direction of his gaze, and, Great Cæsar's Ghost! there under the centre-table I saw my fianceé's cat — a monstrous, masculine cat, as yellow as saffron and ugly as Satan!

"Gentlemen, you would like to know what followed? I cannot tell you. It was bedlam let loose in that beautiful home! My betrothed gave one scream as the dog and cat met, then fainted. I managed to get her out of the room and into the hands of a servant at the other end of the house, and then I went back and looked into the apartment. There was nothing to be seen but revolving remnants of furniture and an atmosphere of yellow and brown which occasionally condensed itself in the centre and then broke again into concentric rings. But I knew what was there nevertheless. I knew that in that yellow and brown atmosphere there were two separate, individual entities, and that they were anatomically hostile and chemically opposite; that sooner or later those two entities would be resolved into their elements or would lie on that floor side by side, dead; and that there would be woe in that house; and that it was no place for me to be found in after the old doctor had returned.

"Under such awful circumstances I left the house. I never went back to it, for the next morning I heard that the doctor had been brought home in a cart, and that distributed resemblances to a cat had been collected and buried in the garden. No tidings reached me of my dog and I believed him to be dead. But I was mistaken. I packed my valise; I started for the train

"THE DOG AND CAT MET."

with the feeling of a man who has lost all and to whom therefore no venture has the terror of a risk. I determined to leave the country forever and come West. For there, I reflected, if anywhere on the earth, amid new scenes, pursuits, and companionship, I should be able to forget the miseries of the past or school myself to endurance.

"With these thoughts in my mind I hurried to the depot, for the whistle of the express had already sounded, and hastily paying for my ticket started for the platform. When,—Great Heavens! what should I see but that irrepressible dog, jauntily trotting across the village Common with his eye open for adventure, and evidently seeking his unfortunate master.

"And this is the reason, gentlemen, why I gave up shooting and became an angler."

At the closing word the signal sounded, the train stopped, under a strong application of the brakes, on the banks of a magnificent stream, which tumbled down from the mountains in a succession of jumps, into wide, deep pools.

"Keep the trout," exclaimed the man gayly, as he swung himself down from the railing, and landed amid wild flowers that bloomed as high as his waist; "keep the trout for your larder; I shall duplicate the string before evening."

"Give us your card," yelled the Judge, as the train started, and he flung his own pasteboard upon the track; "give us your card; how shall I know where to find you next summer?"

"I haven't any card," returned the stranger, calling pleasantly to us as the train receded, "but come next year to the Nepigon and bring all your friends, and you'll find the Man in the Velveteen Jacket on one of the pools."

CHAPTER VI.

THE CAPITALIST.

*Great contest follows and much learned dust
Involves the combatants, each claiming truth,
And Truth disclaiming both.*

ONE of the largest cities on the continent will stand here within fifty years," said the Judge; and he spoke as a man accustomed to know the reasons for his judgment.
This sentence was delivered to our group as we stood on the wharf at Port Arthur, watching the huge steamer, just in from Owen's Sound, unload its monstrous cargo of freight. Its passengers, having landed an hour before, were now rolling west-

ward to the prairies, the mountains, and the shores of the mild ocean.

"I think just as you do," said a gentleman near us; "I think just as you do, sir; and," he added firmly, "I have put up money on my faith."

The voice sounded familiar, very familiar. I glanced at him, but I could not place him for an instant; and then — why, certainly, — the years do change us, — don't they? Gray? of course he should be gray, and I thought of my own head, and, advancing a step, reached out my hand.

"Mr. Pepperell," I said, "I am delighted to greet you; I did not recognize you at first; your hair is whiter than it once was. Every strong stalk flowers at last, eh?"

"I did not recognize you, either," replied Mr. Pepperell, returning my greeting with cordiality. "I did n't recognize you, either, at first, but it was n't because of your whiter head, but because of the bronze on your face. You look like an Indian from the plains."

"I feel like an Indian at least three times a day," I replied; "and the Judge here is making an epicure of me. Mr. Pepperell, allow me to present you to Judge John Doe, of San Francisco," I added. "Judge, this is Mr. Pepperell of Boston, a capitalist of the Hub, and, better than all, a gentleman. I am happy to be the means of bringing you two together." I said it heartily, for I knew them both to be gentlemen of standing, amiability, and wit.

"May I ask, Mr. Pepperell," I said, after he had

been presented to the other members of the party, "may I ask on what grounds you expect a city to be built here in this great opening between the mountains, on the shores of Thunder Bay?"

"The site of great cities," answered Mr. Pepperell,

— and he spoke with that positiveness of expression and breadth of knowledge which characterizes the successful American, — "the site of great cities is a matter of geography. When God formed the continent, he designated where every city on it should be located. Granted a population north and west of Manhattan

Island, and New York must be built. Populate New England, and Boston is the inevitable result. The Lachine Rapids and an inhabited Canada necessitate Montreal. The prairies of the West must have a commercial centre, and hence Chicago. Now look at this site. These mountains, hills, even the islands in front of us, are full of precious ores, — iron, copper (and copper, too, free from sulphur), silver, gold, nickel. Look at this harbor, fenced on all sides from gales, deep, roomy, freed from ice each spring earlier than any other on the lake. Into it empties that river, the Keministiquia, yonder, up whose quiet channel a steamer with a draught of twenty-six feet can steam for four miles. Was there ever such natural wharfage given for commerce, made ready, so to speak, for the hand of man to use, as those eight miles of level river banks? Look at that elevator there. It holds one million, three hundred thousand bushels of wheat. Within sixty days two more of the same size will stand beside it. Four millions of bushels accommodated where two years ago commerce had not laid down a single grain. How many elevators do you think, Judge, will be on that bank ten years from to-day? Last year those prairies to the west produced thirteen million bushels of wheat. This year they will yield twenty millions. Four years ago scientific men were disputing whether wheat would grow on that soil or not! The wheat area west of us is larger than the whole wheat area of the United States. The soil of this vast belt is virgin soil, rich, inexhaustible. I am talking from knowledge, gentlemen. I have been there and looked into this thing, and I know that under decent cultivation every acre will yield forty bushels of finer quality than the wheat of California or Russia. How much wheat do you think will be raised in that vast wheat belt yonder twenty-five years hence? And how is it to reach the markets of the world? It must go south to the States, or it is coming here to Thunder Bay. These are the only two directions it can take in its exit. And so I say, and I've backed my faith with my money, that here on this beautiful site will spring up one of the great cities of the continent."

Mr. Pepperell's presentation of the subject was listened to with the gravest attention by all the group, in which, if the fact must be stated, there was more money seeking investment than is often found on any particular wharf. The Yankee can look up a long perspective with a good dollar at the other end of it, and this northwestern section of the continent is already attracting a deal of attention in the States, from shrewd, far-sighted men.

"Mr. Pepperell," remarked the Judge, "my own judgment, based upon careful forecast, sustains your opinion fully. Illinois is a great State. It is larger in arable acres than England and Wales with their population of twenty-six millions. The State of Illinois can support twenty millions of population easily. But the productive area of this western Canada is ten times larger than the State of Illinois. Two hundred millions of people can be supported, richly supported, north of the forty-ninth parallel. Five hundred miles north of the international boundary you can sow wheat three weeks earlier than you can in Dakota. The climate is milder in the valley of the Peace River than it is in Manitoba. These great facts of Nature are significant and impressive; none the less so because up to this time they have had little advertisement and are known to a comparative few. Yes, sir, you are right; there must be a great city here."

"The fact is," resumed Mr. Pepperell, and he spoke with the enthusiasm which characterizes the American when speaking of his country, "the people of this continent have only just got started. On our side of the line we are sixty millions, which are only the seed of the six hundred millions that are to be. People talk a deal about the capacity of this continent to produce bushels and pounds, grain and meat. Why don't they figure on that higher problem, — the capacity to produce men? Granted a good climate, a productive soil, cheap fuel, absence of war, popularized knowledge, and the ennobling influences of liberty, and what limit can you put to the development of such a people, not in resources alone but in numbers? Why should they not multiply and increase and possess the land? Unless we go to cutting each other's throats, half the present population of the globe will be living on this continent within three hundred years."

"Gad!" said the Judge, "I was born too early!"

"I have a friend," I remarked, "who predicts — and he is n't a Vennor either — that Chicago will ultimately have a population of fifteen millions."

"I have n't a doubt of it," said one of the group, calmly.

"Eh! What!" exclaimed the Judge, "how is it you are so positive?"

"It is a matter of knowledge," returned the man, "absolute knowledge."

"Knowledge!" exclaimed the Judge, "how is that?"

"The gentleman looked at the Judge contemplatively for a few moments, then said, "*I was born there!*"

"O Lord!" exclaimed the Judge, "where's the train?" And breaking up with laughter we started for our car.

No sooner were we on board the train and collected in the smoking room — that most companionable spot for smokers on the earth — than the spirit of the group underwent a characteristic change. With one or two exceptions it happened that we represented the great progressive Republic and that large class of travelers, whose number is legion, that are to-day with lavish expenditures ransacking the globe — a class who go armed with more stories and more cash than the world ever had carried round it before. On the wharf Mr. Pepperell was the impersonation of business ability and foresight; sharp, incisive, edged like a razor, a man whose forecast was that of a statesman and whose language was that of a prince among financiers. With millions to invest, he had on the one hand a full sense of financial responsibility, and on the other, the courage of his judgment. For he had examined the field of his investments for himself, not trusting to the eyes or the words of another, and hence he knew the almost boundless resources of the country and had full faith in its development. But once in the car he was no longer a financier, no longer the business man, no longer the speculator, but an American traveler, jovial, quaint, humorous, vivacious of speech, and loaded to the muzzle with anecdotes.

"You would never suspect, gentlemen, perhaps," said Mr. Pepperell, as he took his cigar from his mouth and blew a dozen rings of blue smoke into the air; "you would never suspect that I was once busted —completely, overwhelmingly busted. In '48 I crossed the plains. I was young. I had an attack of the gold fever — had it bad. I made some money and got a good deal of experience. But on the whole, luck was against me. After ten years of knocking about, during which I was the rolling stone of the proverb, with hundreds of other old time Californians I started for the Fraser. My first experience in British Columbia was at American Bar. below the

Black Cañon, and I shared that magnificent bit of luck with my countrymen. Pushing farther up into the

country — after the Bar had played out — I struck one of the tributaries of the Thompson, pay gravel of the richest sort. I was alone and I decided to work it alone; I had a mule and a billy goat that had followed me when the great camp broke up at American Bar, a hap-hazard impulse on his part probably, for he was the forager of the camp and not a man claimed the least ownership in him. He had probably been lost and won more times at poker than any other bit of property on the face of the earth. Indeed, he was the universal resort of all of us when bankrupted at that lively and fascinating game; for two reasons, — first, because he was no one's property, and second, his value was flexible; it had an elastic quality about it which accommodated the necessities of the man who had lost, and ministered to the amusement of the man who had won. The number of men whom that goat had started on the road to fortune will never be ascertained, and the multitude who, when they had recklessly gambled their last article of value away, with oaths or with laughter claimed one more deal on the strength of that goat as a personal chattel belonging exclusively to themselves, was probably equal to the census of the camp. He had become, therefore, both the inspiration and the consolation of us all; a piece of communal property of accommodating value, which every man, at one time or another, had contemplated with hope or with gratitude; an object of universal solicitude, and of which American Bar was justly proud. His temperament and his habits were such as belonged to his genus. If his animating principle was ever any other than curiosity, surely no one discovered it, and if he ever lost an opportunity to hit a man when a favorable one offered, it never was known. He followed me as my mule ambled out of the camp as he might any other of the six hundred men who were there, and attached himself to my fortunes with that whimsicalness of motive which is probably explainable only to the mind of a goat. His name was Percussion, a name which, with facetious appropriateness, had been given to him by a tall Alabamian one morning immediately after a personal experience by which the name was suddenly suggested,

and which caused the christening to be accompanied with considerable profanity.

"I cannot say that my affections were greatly impressed because Percussion followed me out of the camp, nor did I feel the insinuations of flattery because he thus showed his partiality for my companionship; for I had indisputable evidence that in nature he was wholly void of a conscience, and utterly unable to distinguish between friend and foe. Nor was I deceived by the apparent amiability of his conduct, for during the time he was with me I never dropped my habit of watchfulness, or saw any evidence in the conduct of Percussion that would warrant my doing so. If the old reprobate ever dreamed of reform, the vision of the night never affected in the least the habits of the day.

"You can well imagine," continued Mr. Pepperell, as he lighted a fresh cigar, "that I worked the find for all it was worth. By eking out my provisions with the help of the trout in the stream, I managed to remain in the lonely spot for nearly a month, and then, being absolutely without provisions, I was driven to leave; I was the more willing to do so because, as nearly as I could estimate, I was in possession of fifty thousand dollars' worth of dust and nuggets.

"The last evening I spent in the camp I devoted to arranging for transportation and to picturing the delights of the future. Percussion had not lacked entertainment, for while I was accumulating wealth, he was actively engaged in collecting data for reminiscence. The  white goats of the mountain, so rare south of the national line, were plentiful in the crags around my camp, and more than once had I been amused in contemplating a contest between Percussion and some fac-simile of his of the hills; a contest which I am bound to say invariably terminated in favor of the champion of the camp. It was plainly a case in which civilized training had added to the prowess of nature, and steady practice with a variety of subjects made him master of his art.

"ON A CLIFF, STOOD PERCUSSION."

"I was up with the dawn on the morning set for my departure, and started at once for the little intervale a mile or more distant, where my mule was grazing. I captured it without difficulty, and was in the act of mounting when I heard a noise as of a world rushing to ruin. The earth shook beneath my feet, and the mule trembled with terror. I knew what it meant. I sprang to his back, and  spurred him recklessly up the trail. I reached the brow of the declivity that overlooked the gulch where I had labored. I need not describe what I saw. The face of the mountain to the west had disappeared, and in the place of a mighty forest was a broad tract of bare rock. The Slide had gone down through the gulch, and scoured it to the foundation ledges. The transformation was complete. Not a familiar object was left, save one. On a cliff fifty feet above the spot where my fortune had been found and lost stood Percussion, his tail trembling with excitement and his horns lowered. It was the only opportunity of his life that had passed  unimproved. I called to him to follow me, but he refused to budge. Perhaps he thought another Slide would occur, or had a duel in mind for the morrow. Be that as it may, I left him to his reflections and his engagements, and little thinking that I should ever see him again, I reined my mule down the trail, an utterly despondent man."

In spite of the fact that we were listening to the story of a misfortune that might well overwhelm with despair any person on whom it had fallen, there was not a sober face in the crowd when Mr. Pepperell had brought us to that point of his narration which presented him to us in the most pitiable condition. The awful ruin which the savage Slide had wrought, Percussion on the cliff in the attitude of defiance, the trembling mule and the woe-begone rider thus bereft of his fortune in a minute, — all these we saw as if painted in striking colors on a canvas. And yet, not a face in our group showed the least evidence that we felt ourselves in the presence of disaster.

"I can see," said Mr. Pepperell, as he looked at our faces, "I can see, gentlemen, that you soberly realize the extent of my misfortunes, and appreciate the seriousness of my position. I was *busted*, I tell you, for I started down that trail without a dollar in my pocket or a crust in my saddle-bags. And yet fortune was nigh. For I had not gone a mile down the trail when I came to a small camp in which I found not only needed refreshment but a speculation which brought to me the beginning of my fortune.

"The party into whose camp I had thus fortunately stumbled was one of exploration in the interest of science, and was headed by a scientific man of extraordinary zeal, enormous vanity, vast pretensions, and devoid of common sense.

"Now if there is one class of men I venerate more than others, it is the scientific class. It is true I am not given over much to veneration, for as it happens,

THE PATH OF THE AVALANCHE.

by some arrangement for which I have never been able to feel myself responsible, in that section of my cranium where by rights there should be an eminence, is a kind of prairie flatness, — a dead level as it were. It is consoling to think that I am not answerable for this defect, and I have derived great satisfaction in my life by shuffling it off upon my ancestors, when at times conscience rebuked me at some breach of decorum, or most inappropriate burst of laughter.

" I am happy to reflect that pre-natal influences are answerable for the major part of my weaknesses, and, as I devoutly hope, for the majority of my sins. I sincerely trust that they will be punished as they deserve. The more they catch it, the better my chances appear. I am ready to accept without reserve the harshest dogmas of theology so long as they have no application to myself.

" Nevertheless, in spite of this natural defect in my make-up, I have peculiar feelings toward the average devotee of science. I recognize in him a superior creation. He is the only being I have ever met whose mind seems able to work wholly independent of facts. The facility with which he invents his needed theories fills me with admiration, and the audacity of his imagination in supplying himself with the necessary data for his conclusions is a source of pleasant surprise. It delights me to recall that the most noted leaders of science were certain, a few centuries ago, that the globe was as flat as a shingle; that the whirling earth on which we live had no motion; that the sun, moon, and stars revolved around it as a centre and sum of the great universe; that the blood in the human body stood still; and that the worthy successors of these teachers of accurate knowledge, these men who supplant religion, and substitute knowledge for faith and reason for piety, are now convinced that all the superficial phenomena of the globe, including, of course, the five Great Lakes of this continent, are accounted for by the almost imperceptible and trivial movement of glaciers. Any class of men with such a record receive from me the same overwhelming deference which I involuntarily give to DeFoe, and the author of the 'Arabian Nights.' I yield them the respect and admiration due the chiefest romancers of the race.

"I had no sooner reached his camp than the man of science approached me and made known his mission. It was to capture a specimen of the genuine Rocky Mountain Goat.

"'I am anxious,' he explained, 'to obtain possession, in the interest of science, of a real *Caper Horridus*, in order that I may not only acquire indisputable knowledge of his anatomical structure, but fix beyond peradventure, — and upon this, sir, learned bodies have most differed, — what are his characteristic habits. If you can assist me to obtain a specimen, you will not only be a humble instrument of extending the boundaries of scientific research, but I will remunerate you with the sum which has been put at my disposal by the learned body of men whose president I am, namely, two hundred and fifty dollars in gold.'

"I trust," explained Mr. Pepperell, humbly, "that Heaven has forgiven me for the duplicity of my conduct at that juncture of my fortunes. It was a dreadful temptation. You can see, gentlemen, that it was. I was *busted*. The gentleman wanted a *Caper Horridus*. I knew where he was. He was a genuine *Caper*,

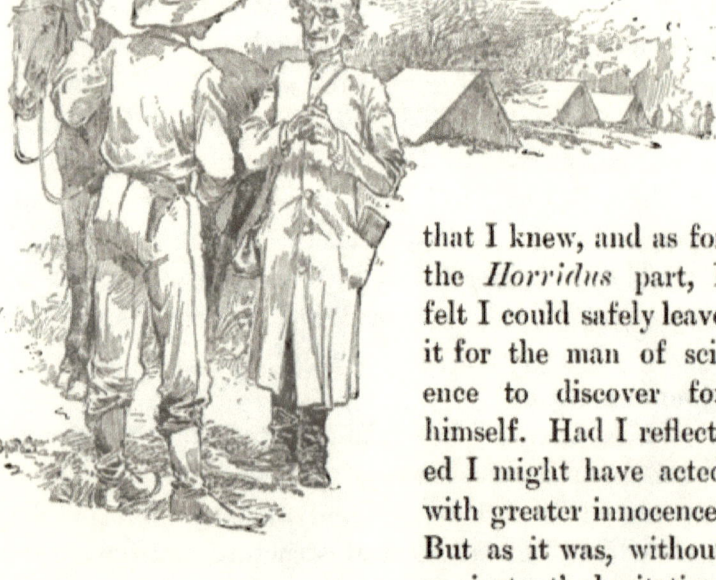

that I knew, and as for the *Horridus* part, I felt I could safely leave it for the man of science to discover for himself. Had I reflected I might have acted with greater innocence. But as it was, without an instant's hesitation, I assured the man of science that I knew where there was a genuine *Caper*; a veritable *Horridus* of the crags, and that I could lead him directly to his habitat. But I distinctly declared I would have nothing to do with the capture of the terrible creature, and that I must be paid my money in advance.

"The man of science was delighted. He paid me the money without an instant's delay, fearing doubtless that I would withdraw my offer or lift my price. He assured me that he needed no assistance; that science had already ascertained that, while excessively curious, the *Caper Horridus* by nature was harmless, and that no hands but his own should make the capture, the fame of which would carry his name round the world.

"You can see, gentlemen, that in the case of two persons animated by motives which inspired both of us, there was no reason for delay. I hitched my mule therefore in position to facilitate mounting, if, as I anticipated, I should return in a hurry, and with the man of science at my heels, proceeded directly up the trail. I did not know exactly where I should find my former companion, but I made no doubt that the old reprobate was still near the path of the Land Slide, and that we should find him in a belligerent mood. And sure enough, we had not gone more than two thirds the distance, when looking carefully over the top of a boulder, standing in an attitude of listening as if anticipating another Slide, there stood Percussion!

"Now as you know, gentlemen, there is a good deal of 'dynamite' in a billy goat. It won't do to drop on to one suddenly unless you wish to be lifted. Any man who runs against a goat suddenly without telegraphing him beforehand, acts as if his business education had been neglected. For a goat is the embodiment of a terrific energy when aroused, and nothing starts him quicker than a sudden appearance. Any man who approaches him without circumspection is liable to lose some part of himself, as it were. More than one man has lost his balance and his self-respect by such carelessness. Both these essentials of standing and character are apt to remain absent during the entire interview.

"A goat is endowed with great quickness of apprehension and he acts on his impulses. When a goat of the masculine gender stands and gazes at you with a look of curious deliberation in his eyes, you will, if you are a rational being, promptly pick the nearest tree and get behind it. This is the only wise course to adopt. Nor should you be slow in doing this. It is not safe to take any chances with a billy goat if he is within fifty feet of you and has in his own mind decided to act. You cannot rely on his remaining where he is any considerable length of time. He is apt to move suddenly, and when he moves he always moves in a straight line, and with his objective point clearly in view.

"To know a goat thoroughly, gentlemen, I am convinced that a man should begin his investigations in childhood. The knowledge needed is not acquired readily by an adult. A man can pilot a steamboat better than a boy, but to steer a goat successfully into a paddock without any back action of the paddles is a feat at which a boy will beat his father every time. The innocent sprightliness of early life is an essential element of success in such an undertaking. A deacon of mature age and dignity of character might do it, but he would never be fit to hold his office after he had finished the job. His record would be broken, as it were. What he had gained in fluency of expression he would have lost in resignation of spirit and the sweet placidness of his vocabulary. A deacon should always leave the management of a billy goat to his hired boy, and keep out of hearing when the boy and the goat are in close communication, too. Any material departure from this rule will always result in unhappiness. The manners of the goat will be spoiled, and the deacon — if the matter be fully reported — will surely lose his office.

"A goat is like any other highly organized creation. He learns evil fast and forgets it slowly. He is a creature of vanity, and relishes success. After he has learned a man's anatomy by experiment, the knowledge is fixed in his mind forever. Time may obliterate the impression he has made on you, but it never obliterates the impression you have made on him. Years may pass; your hairs may be whiter and his coarser, but if he ever gets a chance to hit you again, your years and venerable appearance will not save you. The old reprobate will hit you in the same spot. I have never been able to satisfactorily explain this to my own mind, but the fact remains. I have seen it demonstrated.

"Yes, there stood Percussion. I ducked my head

and beckoned to the man of science. He bounded to my side, and shaking with excitement, peered over the bowlder at him.

"'A *Caper Horridus!*' he gasped. 'A genuine *Caper!* A true *Horridus!*' he exclaimed hoarsely. '*Pedes, nigri; corni, circuli; caput, cornutus; genus, hirsutus; habitus, agilis; homino amicus.*' And fumbling in his pocket for his note-book, he dashed around the bowlder and started for Percussion.

"I cannot describe what followed. Percussion was at his best or his worst that morning. He had missed one great opportunity, and was in no mood to be trifled with. He struck the man of science at the precise spot selected in his own mind, and with the force of a catapult. He bowled him past the point of rock behind which I was crouched as if he had been a packbasket. His impetus brought him within sight and he came at me as if I was a land slide.

"'You miserable cuss,' I exclaimed, 'don't you know your benefactor?' And I went up a tree. I yelled to the man of science to light out. He recovered his breath and his legs at the same time and ricochetted down the trail as if fired out of a columbiad, yelling, 'Caper Horridus!' 'Caper Horridus!' at every jump.

"After him bounded Percussion. Without an instant of hesitation I followed. I had a longing to get on to my mule. The man of science reached the edge of the camp and fell flat, and Percussion struck a Chinook Indian in a way to increase his vocabulary. The last jump I made carried me to the back of my mule, and I tore down the trail with my heels in her flanks. I reached the banks of the Thompson and went in at a jump. Half across the flood I heard a fusilade and I knew that Percussion had at last struck a land slide."

"Rat Portage, gentlemen!" called the conductor. "Twenty minutes to see the Lake of the Woods and the great flour mill at Kewatin!"

CHAPTER VII.

A JOLLY CAMP AT RUSH LAKE.

"Nature's prime favorites we the Pelicans,
High-fed, long-lived, sociable and free."

"HEAVENS!" exclaimed Mr. Pepperell. "Judge, look at those prairie chickens!" We had stepped from the cars at Winnipeg, and as we struck the platform we found ourselves in front of a heap of grouse, — a hundred in number, it may be, — big, fat birds, such as make man thankful he was born with a stomach. The Judge looked at the birds. There was a wistful look in his eyes. His lips moved as if the gamey flavor were already in his mouth. He rolled his eyes toward me longingly, and queried, —

"Where did those birds come from?"

"From Southern Manitoba," I answered promptly. "They are as thick as grasshoppers there."

The Man from New Hampshire had been fumbling at the birds, as if examining their condition, and when he lifted one, lo! there was a tag tied to its foot, and on the tag was penciled, "Colonel Goffe, New Hampshire."

"One of my birds, by gosh!" said the Colonel.

"Clean from your farm, eh, Colonel?" exclaimed Mr. Pepperell.

"Certainly," returned the Colonel; "flew straight to this platform and dropped dead. Knew I was to be here. I'll eat him to-night," and he passed the bird in under his arm between his coat and his vest.

"My conscience! My conscience!" groaned the Judge, as if wrestling with an internal enemy. "The gods have burdened me with a conscience."

"My bird! My bird!" returned the New Hampshire man, groaning in imitation of the Judge. "The gods have burdened me with a bird," and he started for the car.

"Halloo, old boy!" screamed a voice, and a flat hand smote me on the back. "Do you remember the turkeys in Texas?"

"Yes," I answered, as I wheeled, "and that the best snap shot in the New York Gun Club, Jack Osgood by name, could n't hit a turkey gobbler at fifty feet as he went through the live oaks." And we shook hands, laughed, and roared, as two sportsmen will when they suddenly meet, with years between them and some ludicrous happening.

"Jack Osgood, — Judge Doe, — Mr. Pepperell," I said, briefly introducing them. "We shot turkeys together in Texas," I added.

"He shot them, and I shot at them," replied Jack. "I never shall forget how I felt when the first gobbler got up ahead of my gun. I shook till my bones rattled; it took me two days to sober down and get steady."

"Did you shoot those birds there, Mr. Osgood?" asked the Judge.

"Certainly; every one of them, sir," answered Jack. "I dropped them for four bags. There are ninety-seven all told. If you want any, help yourselves, gentlemen. You will find them good broilers."

"Heaven has not forsaken me!" exclaimed the Judge, as he fingered the breast of a chicken, and liking the one he had so well, he took another.

"I'm not mean enough to look a gift horse in the mouth, Judge," said Mr. Pepperell, and he carelessly picked up *three* chickens.

"Where are you going, Jack?" I queried.

"I am going to Rush Lake, after canvas-backs," replied Osgood.

"What did you say, Mr. Osgood?" exclaimed the Judge. "What was the *name* you gave to the ducks?"

"Canvas-backs, sir," answered Jack.

"Gentlemen," exclaimed the Judge, "I don't know how you feel, but I'm tired of traveling. This steady rolling shakes up a man of my age terribly. If Mr. Osgood will permit, I will go to Rush Lake with him. I feel that my system requires several days of absolute rest."

"I dare not leave you to go alone, Judge," cried the Man from New Hampshire, who was leaning from the platform of the car, listening to what the Judge said. "Your conscience! think of your conscience. *Where did you get those two chickens?*" and he glared at the Judge enviously.

And so it was arranged that we should all drop off at Rush Lake, and have a few days with the canvas-backs and the white pelicans, and we started out under the guidance of Osgood to get together our supplies.

"Ten years ago," remarked Mr. Pepperell, "there were not a hundred white people here. At the forks of the river was Old Fort Garry, a Hudson Bay Company's post, and that was all. To-day there is a city solidly built of brick and stone, with a population of thirty thousand. It is necessary to see such changes with our eyes to appreciate them."

"It looks to me as if it had a future," said the Judge; "a great future."

"Decidedly," answered Mr. Pepperell. "This is to be the Prairie City, as Vancouver is to be the Coast City of the country. The one will be built up by the inland trade; the other by its foreign commerce."

"Winnipeg will have rivals to the west, Mr. Pepperell, and don't you forget it in your figuring," observed the Man from New Hampshire.

A BLIND SQUAW ON A HORSE.

"I don't forget it," returned Mr. Pepperell, promptly. "I have counted on it. But Winnipeg has the start, a good strong start, over every rival to the west or east. Her thoroughfares are constructed; her system of lighting in operation; her water-works provided; her public buildings erected; her wholesale and retail houses established, and her trade connections with the East and the South made, Colonel Goffe. A financier knows the value of such a start. Winnipeg has got her grip on the country round about her, and it will take an earthquake or a cyclone to loosen it."

And so, like active-minded Americans, while buying our supplies and getting together our outfit for the camp at Rush Lake, we talked of the future of Winnipeg and figured on its changes.

If there are prettier bits of water anywhere than can be found in these Western prairies, they have not been discovered. A few are alkaline, but many are fresh, and the prairies roll down in billows of grass to their beaches or flatten to the water through acres of sedge. Rush Lake is well named, and yet it is not swampy nor sluggish; for miles of its shore line are embanked, and its waters are lively. From these banks the prairie rolls away in waves of fine verdure, and the eye sweeps unimpeded to the rim of the horizon. Our tent was pitched on a bank which brought the lake in full view, and over it the air moved in cool, easy currents. It was an ideal camp for a sportsman, for the free water was speckled with ducks, and the vast reedy spaces were alive with their movements.

Canvas-backs, mallards, teal, black ducks, wood

ducks, curlew, the big plover, and those wonders of the western land, the huge snow-white pelicans, whose wings have the stretch of a white-headed eagle's, and which float on the water with the slow, stately movement of swans, — all were here, and in numbers beyond counting. On the prairie were coyotes, gray wolves, and antelopes. What more could a sportsman desire than such a camp and such game?

"Heavens!" cried the Judge, "was there ever such music?" and he tumbled off his cot.

"A chorus for the saints," replied the New Hampshire man, as he emerged from the folds of a buffalo robe in which he had bestowed himself near the tent-pins; and in less than a minute we were all standing outside of the tent completing our toilet, the Judge with one boot in his hand, and Mr. Pepperell discreetly wrapped in a blanket. What a morning!

The sun had not yet risen. One great star, a globe of liquid luminance, hung in the eastern sky. Along the horizon's edge ran a line of rose. Above it were the shifting splendors of an oriental ruby. The western heavens were still blue black. The prairie grasses were wet with dew, and every drooping point sparkled like a gem. The air was motionless, and the lake from shore to shore was blanketed with white fleece. And out of this fleece, what noises came! The flutter of plumes; the spatter of playful ducks; the pipe of curlew and plover; the whiz of passing wings; the voice of pelican; the honk of geese; the low soft sound of feathery life, seeking, feeding, greeting, filled all the air with murmurous musical sounds.

"Oh, the glory of the world! — the glory of the world!" cried the Judge, as he gazed at the beauty and breathed the pure air in.

"Oh, the glory of the ducks! — the glory of the ducks!" said the Man from New Hampshire, as he listened to the sounds in the fog and thought of the broiled grouse that he ate for his supper.

"Osgood," I said, "did a sportsman ever hear sweeter music?"

"Never," he responded, "unless it was the gobble of a wild turkey as he strutted in front of his harem in some little glade among the cedar groves of the Guadaloupe."

"Is that coffee I smell?" queried Mr. Pepperell, suddenly.

"It is, by the powers!" exclaimed the Judge, and he dove through the door of the tent to complete his toilet.

"That Judge of ours," said the Man from New Hampshire, pointing to the door of the tent as he disappeared, — "that Judge of ours is a good deal of a poet, but he has a well-balanced mind notwithstanding."

"Cook," called the Judge, as he thrust his head out of the tent in the direction of the kitchen. "Cook, how soon will breakfast be ready?"

"In a few minits, Marse Judge, in a few minits," responded the darkey.

"Julius Cæsar Bismarck!" thundered the Judge. "At what *hour*, I say, will you have breakfast ready?"

"Fo' de Lawd, Marse Judge," promptly replied the ebony cross between ancient and modern greatness, "how d' you s'pose dis nigger knows?"

"Oh Lord!" groaned the Judge, and his voice sounded as if it came from an empty cellar.

"Why do you move so carefully?" asked Mr. Pepperell of the New Hampshire man, as ready for breakfast we went out of the tent.

"Sh!" returned the Man from New Hampshire. "If I don't move carefully the Judge will hear me rattle."

With the dawn the lake shore near us had been embellished with a most romantic arrival. A tribe of the Blackfeet Nation had come in from the plains and gone into camp. Twenty-six large, fine-looking Tepees were stretched in a row to the east and north of our tent, and some hundred and fifty Indian men, women, and children were grouped round their camp-kettles or moving about at their work. Here and there stood knots of men picturesquely draped in their blankets of high colors. These Indians were not vagabonds, nor sots; they were not bloated with liquor, nor broken down with disease; they were not dirty or repulsive to the eye; they were fine, healthy-looking people. The men were tall and well formed, the boys sprightly in their motions. The squaws did not look like drudges or human beasts of burden, but like women of bronze skin, living the life and doing the work of aboriginals; they were all comfortably clothed, and some of the girls were finely formed and unmistakably handsome. There was not a half-breed among them. It was a camp of full-blooded Indians of the plains.

"Gentlemen," said the Judge, "if I ever lose my appetite I shall come to Rush Lake."

AN INDIAN GIRL IN A WHEAT FIELD.

"If Canada ever loses Rush Lake, then," retorted the Man from New Hampshire, "I shall know where to look for it;" and he measured with his eye the front elevation of the Judge.

"Gentlemen," exclaimed the Judge, ignoring the remark of the New Hampshire man, "I wish it understood that this is a camp of sportsmen, and not pot-hunters. We are not here to make money, but to spend it; not to supply the market, but ourselves with game, and therefore I move that we act like true sportsmen, and fix the size of our bags each day by mutual agreement. Friends should be remembered," continued the Judge, "and I suggest that each man be permitted to kill a certain number of ducks for himself, and a certain number to send to his friends."

"I move," suggested Mr. Pepperell, "that every man be permitted to shoot twelve ducks and two pelicans during the week for himself."

"What about plover and curlew?" queried Osgood.

"They don't count," decided the Judge. "You can bag all you can."

"Don't count!" exclaimed the Man from New Hampshire. "That decision would n't stand a minute in the highest court. I know a man in Texas who started in to eat fifty-six curlew, and when he got to the forty-second he dropped" —

"Stop right there, sir," said the Judge, shaking his finger at the Colonel. "Stop right there! The court has n't forgotten your story of the Japanese screen. The number being settled that each man may shoot for himself, it only remains for us to decide how many he may be allowed to shoot for his friends."

"I would like to shoot a dozen a day for my friends," said Mr. Pepperell. "The station isn't a mile away, and we can start them east every evening."

"That will do for me," added Osgood, cheerfully. "If it gets a little dull, I'll try my hand at the antelopes and the wolves."

"I'm not a shot-gun man, and will live on your bounty," I remarked. "If you'll give my Winchester a pelican each day, and full swing at the wolves and coyotes, I shall have a royal time."

"Well, sir," queried the Judge of the Colonel, "how many do you want for your friends?"

"I haven't an enemy in the State," said the Man from New Hampshire, "and by the last census" —

"Colonel Goffe!" interrupted the Judge, sternly, "the court will not be trifled with. How many do you want for your friends?"

"Well, as I was saying," said the Colonel, "I haven't an enemy in the State of New Hampshire, and the last census fixed the population at three hundred and fifty thousand. Of this number only seventy thousand are voters. I wouldn't give a duck to a Democrat if I died for it, so we can chalk off" —

"Colonel Goffe," thundered the Judge, "the court does not propose to sit on this camp-stool all day, and if you don't come down" —

"Oh, very well, very well," cried the Colonel, "it is not good politics to leave out New Hampshire in any close election, but let her go. Outside of New Hampshire I've only one friend. I picked him up this morning; he's herding the Indian ponies out there,

A JOLLY CAMP AT RUSH LAKE.

and he looked to me as if he had n't had duck for some time, and that he would prove mighty elastic when he got duck"—

"Gentlemen," exclaimed the Judge, interrupting the Colonel, "our friend from New Hampshire has suggested a most amiable settlement of the question. We will abide by our ruling, and the Colonel shall be free to shoot as many ducks as he can for the Indians." And with this decision we all arose, well pleased, and went for our guns.

Now the Man from New Hampshire was a wag, dry as seasoned hickory. Luck invariably assists such a man when bent on a joke, and luck had assisted this gray-headed joker to such an armament as many readers of this book, I am sure, never saw. In a gun-shop at Winnipeg, he had found an old-fashioned flintlock, known among our forefathers as a king's arm. It was of monstrous bore, thick at the breech and thin at the muzzle; with a strong stock mounted heavily in solid brass, and an iron ramrod. The flint was half the size of a small fire shovel, while the pan was as large as an iron spoon.

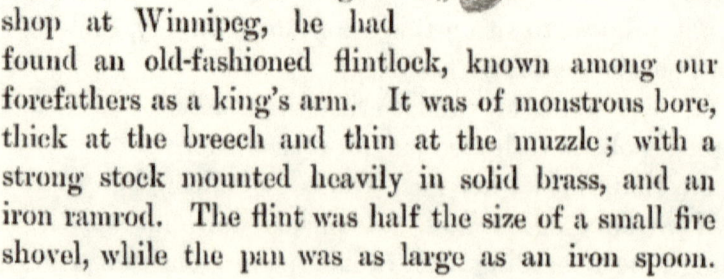

It was a venerable relic of former days and men; a murderous old gun, if you had shot and powder enough to charge it properly, and you could ever get it off; but most eccentric and unreliable in its habits. The gun was apparently strong as ever, and as to its barrel, in good repair, but the lock was lashed to its place by stout leather thongs, and unless the powder was coarse, the grains would leak through between the barrel and the pan into the recess where the springs and tumbler were located. The spectacle which the Colonel presented when he stood equipped for the day, — a big powder horn with a wooden stopple under his elbow, one pocket sagging with shot, the other stuffed full of oakum and paper for his wadding, the old gun in his hand, and a white bell-crowned hat on his head, which he had found by the same luck that got him his gun, was of so funny a sort that the camp roared with laughter. But the Colonel took the jokes that we fired at him with imperturbable gravity, and we knew that if ever he did get that old gun off, and there were any ducks in the landscape within range, the Indian encampment would be fed full to feasting.

In less than an hour each of us had his bag except the Colonel. "For some unexplainable reason," as he stated, he had been "unable to get the old thing off." But he assured us he had confidence in his piece, and that sooner or later the world would hear from him. There was not one of us that did not admire both his courage and perseverance, for he stood bravely up behind the old mortar and pulled the trigger at every duck that came by.

"Lord!" said the Judge, "what would become of the Colonel if the old thing should go off?" So we patiently trailed in the rear of his canoe in response to the Colonel's exhortation, "to stand by the institution of the fathers." Advice and interrogations were rained upon him. The Judge wanted to know "if he had loaded every time he snapped, and if he knew how many charges there were in the piece?" Mr. Pepperell inquired "if he had powder enough to keep on priming for the rest of the day?" And Osgood suggested that we each "take our turn and spell him at pulling the trigger."

Meanwhile, as we had stopped shooting, the ducks had settled thicker and thicker, till the water was black and the sedge was full of feathers, and the Colonel worked away at the ancient bit of machinery with redoubled vigor. He who says that the age of miracles has passed is an idiot, for that old gun finally went off — went off at an opportune moment too, for the canoe was wedged into the sedge, the Colonel well braced, and the air filled with ducks. Granted the air black with birds; an old king's arm charged with a gill or more of coarse shot, and a man from New Hampshire squinting grimly over the breech-pin, and there could be but one result, or rather three results. The gun jumped out of his hands, the Colonel sat down in the boat with a crash, and ducks fell by the dozen. It was a monstrous bag in truth, and the Colonel took the honors of the day and week, for while he averaged less than five shots a day, still the totals beat every gun in the crowd. One thing is sure, the Indians who camped with us on Rush Lake that week will never forget that old flintlock gun or the Man from New Hampshire, nor shall we who were there ever forget the sport and the fun.

CHAPTER VIII.

BIG GAME.

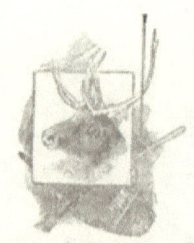

"HAVE hunted every kind of game between the Southern Gulf and Great Slave Lake," replied Mr. Osgood, in answer to an interrogation from Colonel Goffe, as we were sitting, one evening, in front of our tent at Rush Lake, "and I can give you as much or as little information as you wish on the subject of big or little game, bird or beast. Twenty years ago the big game of the continent could be found north or south of the international line, and even ten years back good hunting could be had in several of our States and Territories, but to-day he who wishes to find game of the larger sort, many kinds and plenty of it, must come over on this side of the line and hunt northward."

"What do you mean by northward, Jack?" I asked. "How far north have you hunted?"

"Six hundred miles at least, perhaps eight," he answered. "Last summer I started from Calgary with a

comrade, and fetched a trail on horseback well down into the great Mackenzie Basin. The Mackenzie, you know, is a mighty river, bigger than the Mississippi, they say, and the country it drains is an empire in itself."

"That is a long way to go for a hunt, Jack," I said, interrupting him.

"You and I trailed farther than that south and west," he retorted pleasantly. "But you must remember, gentlemen, that from the hour you leave Cal-

WHITE TAIL DEER.

gary you are in good sporting country. We hugged the foot-hills from the start, and we had bighorn, goats, bear, antelopes, and wolves with which to amuse ourselves. Then you must remember that we were in the saddle, and trailing through a most lovely country, without weariness and at no burdensome expense, pushing up into a strange region known only to the Indians and the Hudson Bay Post folk, through an atmosphere pure and bracing as men ever rode in. I assure you that had I not fired my rifle from beginning to end of it, that two months' trail would have been most enjoyable."

"What is the character of the soil and climate in this North Land of yours, Mr. Osgood?" queried the Judge.

"The soil is as rich as any on the continent," answered Jack, "and the climate simply perfect. It is milder than it is here, or even in Dakota or Minnesota. Wheat can be sown earlier — three weeks earlier, I should think — than at the national line. The days are longer, and the cereal growths get the benefit of the prolonged solar light; a great benefit, I can assure you, it is in bringing a crop along fast. At the northern part of my trail I could read a newspaper at midnight without the aid of candle or moon. It is Daylight Land up there, and so it might, in truth as well as in poetry, be called."

"That is a beautiful name," cried the Judge enthusiastically. "A beautiful name! Daylight Land! That is n't much like the popular conception of Canada, which pictures it as the home of Ice and of Night. I verily believe that half the world thinks of Canada as a cold, desolate country the year round."

"The world knows nothing about Canada as a whole," Jack replied warmly. "Nor do Canadians in general know anything of their own country. They are not travellers, as we Yankees are. The old French

stock were great wanderers and explorers, but their descendants are stay-at-homes. The old-time French Canadians went everywhere. The grandsire was a *voyageur;* his descendants to-day are only *habitans.* He fed his sinews on the game of the whole continent. These eat pease and garlic at home. The fact is Canada knows less of herself than she did a century and a half ago. She is absolutely engaged in rediscovering her own geography. The same thing is happening in Canada, touching her great rivers, lakes, and fertile plains, as happened in Italy in respect to Pompeii and Herculaneum. They are being uncovered and brought to the light. They have lain buried under a huge deposit of ignorance, and are now being exhumed. There are a dozen American sportsmen I could mention who know more about Canada than the Geographical Department at Ottawa."

"Why, Jack," I exclaimed, "you are quite an orator. The Canadian government ought to put you on a salary to write their advertising literature and make immigration speeches."

"You can laugh as much as you like," returned Jack with good-natured earnestness, "but you know I am right, for you know as much of this great country as I do, and perhaps more. I wish our countrymen would learn the facts about this huge empire of opportunity to the north of them, or that the Canadians had knowledge of it themselves, faith in it, and the right connections with us. Then you would see this western land jump to the front of continental observation."

"I don't see where the immigration is to be found to people this vast country," said Colonel Goffe. "The United States have thus far preëmpted the immigration possibilities of the world, and stand intermediate between the great western movement of population which signalizes our age, and this country, and I can't see how this Canada of the west and northwest is ever to be peopled. A goodly number of English and Scotch are already here, but it will take many years of such slow additions to people these vast areas which stretch west and north from this spot."

"The people to populate this country," said Jack, "are coming from Great Britain, the north of Europe, and perhaps from the States. Americans as well as Europeans should possess this land. This country is agricultural, and in a few years a great agricultural movement from the States northward is likely to take

place. Our tent is pitched at the centre of the wheat area of the continent. Five hundred miles to the north and as far to the south from where we sit, and a thousand miles east and west, measure what I call the great wheat square of the continent. Here is pure water, a perfect climate, cheap fuel, and a soil that produces forty bushels of prime wheat to the acre. As the soil to the south under our silly system of agriculture becomes exhausted, as it soon will be, and the average yield per acre shrinks more and more, the wheat growers must and will move northward. This movement is sure to come. It is one of the fixed facts of the future; it is born of an agricultural necessity, and when it begins to move it will move in with a rush. A million of American wheat farmers ought to be in this country inside of ten years, and I believe that within that time population will pour in and spread over these Canadian plains like a tide."

"Jack Osgood," I exclaimed, "you are the same sanguine theorist that you were eight years ago. You came to Texas to shoot turkeys for a month, and before half the month had passed you bought twenty thousand acres of land."

"So I did," he rejoined, "and I beg you to remember that I paid one dollar and twenty-five cents per acre, and that I sold out last year, as you know, for eight dollars and fifty cents per acre. It pays to be a theorist in an age and country like this."

"Mr. Osgood," said the Man from New Hampshire, "I am convinced that you and I are adapted to do business as partners. If you can select twenty thousand acres anywhere around here that look as those twenty thousand you bought in Texas did, I will go halves with you, and we will stake out a city near the centre of the section at once."

"Come, come," I said when the laughter had subsided, "have done with this enthusiastic forecast and your speculative talk, and tell me about the big game, as you promised to do at the start. How far north did you go, Jack, and what did you find in the way of game?"

"I went as far as the Great Slave Lake. The shores of this lake are the favorite haunt of the musk ox, and I wanted to get some of the strange-looking creatures. You can find them on all the upper tributaries of the Mackenzie River. A musk ox is a sizable game, for the males weigh four or five hundred pounds, and the

females nearly as much. They are about eight feet long and four high, and have a dark amber-colored coat. In the fall of the year they grow a very fine wool. They have a flat frontal, and the horns, which are very large at the base, grow out of the top of the skull close to each other, and curve downward on either side of the head, but turn sharply upward some six inches from the ends, and are finely pointed. They seem to me to resemble a sheep more than an ox, but they do

PRONG HORN ANTELOPE.

not have the cry of a sheep or goat, but make a noise like to the snort of a walrus. They signal danger by stamping like a buck, or by striking their horns against the horns of others standing near. They are courageous, and fight savagely. Even bears are killed by them. The calf is a feeble thing, and can't follow the mother for a month or more after birth. The mothers hide their calves very cunningly, and protect them with the utmost affection. They feed on grasses, mosses, and browse, and their flesh tastes very like moose-meat or venison, only it is of a coarser grain. They are shy, and keep sentinels well out from the herd when feeding, and hence it is good sport to stalk them. I spent a week hunting them, and had good success; but I had more enjoyment in watching them and studying their habits than in killing them, for after I had collected a few specimen skins I had no motive to kill farther."

"That's right," said the Judge. "Boys are murderous chaps with the gun, but when a man has shot a few years he begins to shoot less and study more, and finds more pleasure in learning than in killing. A true sportsman becomes, as he grows in years and skill, more and more a naturalist, and receives more pleasure from the living knowledge he acquires than the dead game he bags."

"The caribou are very plenty in the north," resumed Jack. "There are two varieties, the woodland and the barren-ground caribou. They are found in large herds around Athabaska Lake and southward of Hudson's Bay to Lake Superior. I need not describe them to you, for you have all, doubtless, seen them. In summer they come from the far north, and feed around James's Bay. The caribou are good game, for it takes skill, patience, and physical endurance to stalk one successfully. When he finds himself hunted, he travels with a low head, his antlers well back, and

keeps his body close to the ground. I followed one on the Nelson River four days before I captured him, and he came near bagging me instead of I him, for I only wounded him, and he charged at me like an elephant. The barren-ground caribou is not much known, I fancy, among the sportsmen of the States. They are much smaller than the woodland species, weighing only about one hundred pounds when dressed. They are very plenty in the Great Slave and Athabaska Lake region. Small as they are, their antlers are much larger than those of the larger species. They have more branches on them, and are far handsomer. In summer they are a reddish brown, but in winter almost snow white. The skin tans finely, becoming very soft and white, and is used for tents and garments. Their flesh is excellent, and the fat on the rump is highly prized as a great delicacy by the Indians and French *voyageurs*. It is not difficult to stalk them, as they are not shy as is the larger kind, and hence it is not much sport to hunt them. I have seen a hundred or more in a herd."

"Are the buffalo actually gone, Mr. Osgood?" queried the Judge.

"I saw three within fifty miles of Calgary, last year," Jack answered. "I did not kill them, of course. I dare say they have been killed since. I have a feeling that a few might yet be found by searching among the foot-hills northwest of us, and I saw a living trail last summer in the Peace River country, but the buffalo of the plains is practically an extinct animal. There is a family or tribe of buffalo, known as the wood buffalo, to the north of us, however."

"I never heard of them before," remarked Mr. Pepperell.

"Very likely," said Jack. "I never did until I heard of them from the Indians north of Edmonton last year. There are not more than a thousand all told, perhaps, but they are noble animals, and the sportsman that captures one has a trophy of which he may well be proud. The wood buffalo is much larger and handsomer than his brother of the plains. His hair is finer, and his great size makes him a nobler object to look at. He lives wholly in the forest, and is very wild and hard to get at. But a real sportsman would gladly ride a thousand miles to get a good shot at one. I have two skins at home, and I prize them as trophies of the chase beyond any others that twenty years of hunting all over the continent have given me."

"Are there many Rocky Mountain goats in this Canadian country?" I asked.

"Plenty of them everywhere in the mountains," he answered. "South of the national line they are not very plenty, but as you travel northward they become more and more numerous. You will, I presume, see them from the car window as you ride along, once you get into the mountain section to the west of us. I see they have been represented as very shy and difficult to stalk, by a prominent sportsman of the States. I have not found this to be the case after I had studied their habits and character a little. The first thing to remember in stalking a white goat is that he is by nature a most curious animal. His bump of inquisitiveness is excessively large. You must not attempt to stalk him too much. You must let him stalk you. If you move he will see you, and away he goes at a bound; but if you don't move, but remain hidden and expose something to his sight that he does not understand, and exercise patience, it is ten to one that in half an hour you have drawn him within range. Indeed, the true rule in any form of hunting is to move very little and very slowly, or not at all. The adage that 'luck comes to the man who won't go after it,' is especially verified in stalking. I have killed more game by sitting still than by tramping or riding after it."

"In the second place I made a very interesting discovery, and I made it by accident, one day. I was stalking a fine old billy goat in the mountains north of Bow River with a comrade, a green man, who did n't seem to have an eye in his head. The game was above me, half a mile away, perhaps, and I was moving up with the utmost circumspection, when to my dismay I saw my comrade suddenly emerge from the scrub five hundred feet above the old fellow, and walk carelessly along in full view. I was not surprised that my friend did not see the goat, for I doubt if he would have seen an elephant twenty rods in front of him, but I was surprised that the goat did n't see him, for he was a foxy old chap, and kept his eyes open. And then it was that I suddenly made a discovery, — a discovery which made goat-stalking easy to me after that, — which was that a goat never expects danger from above, but always from below, and that to stalk a mountain where goats are, successfully, the stalker should work downward from the top, and not upward from the base.

"It is just the same with big horn sheep, as they are called. They should be stalked from above. They have a wide range, for I have shot them in Southern California and in the Great Bear Lake region. They are not confined to the mountains, as is generally supposed. I have found them in flat country, and thick too. They live in Sonora, in tracts absolutely arid; at least I never could find any water there. A ram weighs, when fully grown and well conditioned, about three hundred and fifty pounds. They grow a very fine wool in winter, and the females have horns like a common goat. The old idea that they alight on their big horns when compelled to jump from a cliff is all nonsense. It is like the popular belief that prairie dogs, owls, and rattlesnakes live in one burrow harmoniously. There is no such 'happy family' arrangement among them, I can assure you. The snakes eat the eggs of the owls, the owls eat the snakes, and the prairie dogs eat the owl chicks at every opportunity. A good many men with big-sounding titles would be much better naturalists if they would become practical sportsmen and trailers for a few years."

"That's my idea, Mr. Osgood," said the Judge,

ROCKY MOUNTAIN SHEEP.

with strong emphasis. "If I had a boy and I wanted to make a true naturalist of him, I would buy him a sportsman's outfit and give him to you for five years to educate."

"Well, I could teach him a good many valuable things, I don't doubt, or any other true sportsman could who has trailed the continent as widely as I have," Jack responded. "For he would see not only its physical geography and its old races, now almost extinct, but all its vegetable and arboreal growths, and above all learn how to use his eyes and his ears and his reasoning faculties more sharply and carefully than he could in the recitation room of a college. Mr. Murray and I were graduated from Yale, and we remember our Alma Mater with scholarly gratitude, but the Great University of Men and Things, as represented by our studentship of the continent, has given us a more valuable knowledge than our study of books ever did."

"Never mind that now, Jack," I said; "you and I can't graduate from the big Outdoor University until we have saddled across the Mackenzie Basin and boated down its current a thousand miles, or two thousand, for that matter."

"I will do that with you any summer," he said. "Three months will be all the time we need, and from the day we leave Calgary till our return we shall be in the best hunting region of the continent — the section where big game in abundance and all its varieties, excepting the plain buffalo, can now be found. All through this area north of us the wapiti, or big elk, are found plentifully, both among the foot-hills and in the woody clumps and timber which patch the plains of the country here and there. The wapiti are noble game, and the stalking of them a most manly recreation. As to grizzlies, I never hunt them. I do not admit that a sportsman has such a motive in his sporting adventures as to justify him in risking his life, as he must do in stalking for grizzlies. Mr. Murray saw me run from a grizzly once, and I am confident that he never saw a man of my inches make better time. I have killed two, but in both instances I was so placed that I could n't run, and had to kill or get killed, so I stood stoutly in for the chances, and won. There are two animals I never seek, and always shun if I can : the grizzly bear and the panther. The latter is the king of the American forest and mountains. He is the only beast the grizzly fears. The lithe cat is more than a match for the monstrous bear. The Indians will tell you that they have found many grizzlies that were certainly killed by panthers, but no one has ever seen the body of a panther that was killed by a grizzly or any other animal. The panther is king of the woods.

"Moose are numerous in the Peace River country, among the mountains and on the west side of the mountains. It has been said that no white man can hunt a moose as well as an Indian. As a rule the saying holds good. To it I have known a few exceptions, but only a few. The influence of heredity is in the Indian's favor. His eyesight is a derived faculty. It is a birthmark. The Indian's eye has ancestors back of it. A thousand years of practiced, developed vision

THE GRIZZLY BEAR.

is concentrated, and peers from under his brows. The aboriginal eye is the best in the world. It is literally microscopic. In moose-stalking this counts. The stalker who can stalk without noise, and whose eye is as good or better than the moose's, gets him every time. The eye wins in moose-hunting.

"Antelopes are not game. They are too pretty to

shoot, and too simple. Their curiosity is so enormous that it dominates them. It places them entirely at the mercy of the sportsman, and hence every true sportsman spares the lovely creatures, unless absolutely compelled to kill to appease his hunger. But the big gray wolf is legitimate game, and the great, gaunt, hulking brute makes a good target; and his pelt is not to be despised, for when full furred it looks well, and a dozen of them make a warm robe, or overcoat even. These wolves are everywhere to the north of us, and often make good sport as you trail onward.

"The reason why the great area north of us is to be commended to the American sportsman," said Jack in conclusion, "is because it is the present home of the big game of the continent, and is accessible. The rails bring you to your saddle, and the saddle takes you to the end of your trail. And after my way of thinking there is no method of locomotion so healthy, so stimulating, and so thoroughly enjoyable, as you have with a good, tough, easy-gaited, well-trained pony under you, trailing over the great plains. Pushing down toward the north from Calgary you have the prairie land to the east and the Rocky Mountains to the west in full view; grasses and flowers, running streams and groves of trees, pure air and lovely camp grounds; a climate of even temperature, long, lingering twilights and early dawns, and that most delightful of all sensations to a trailer,— the feeling that you are visiting an unknown section without danger or excessive toil, and in which game is abundant. Even if you cared nothing for game, and were only seeking a glorious outing, I can imagine no excursion likely to yield more health or pleasure to a party of refined and intelligent lovers of the outdoor world and life than one pushed down toward the north into the Peace River country from Calgary, keeping the snowy summits of the Rocky Mountains in sight on the left as you journey along. Granted a good-sized 'prairie schooner,' a good cook, a good teamster, and a good party, and after my way of thinking you have all the conditions of a good time."

"So say I," cried the Judge, as he rose to his feet and extracted a small package from his coat pocket, "and I wish we boys could all start on such a journey tomorrow. But one thing, Colonel Goffe, you could not do. The court would not allow it; you should never be permitted to take that old combination musket of yours along. It is more dangerous than a 'sugar trust,'" and the Judge proceeded to open the package in his hand, which proved to contain nothing but small oblong pieces of pasteboard with grotesque pictures upon them.

"Judge John Doe, what are those things you have in your hands?" exclaimed the Colonel, in a severe voice. "They look to me like a pagan cryptogram, and if Mr. Ignatius Donnelly gets hold of you" —

"That will do," interrupted the Judge coolly, as he began to move his fingers up and down over the package in a manner to make the slips of paper come and go in a strange fashion, "that will do. Colonel Goffe," he added as he prepared to sit down on his camp-stool, "these are cards, sir. This is a poker pack, and in spite of your innocence I propose that you and I should have a game" —

"Sit down, Judge," said the Colonel kindly, as he moved the Judge's stool a little closer to him.

"Thank you, Colonel," replied the Judge, in a mollified voice, evidently touched by the Colonel's courtesy. "I will sit down," and he did — on the grass!

"*You villain!*" screamed the Judge, and jumping to his feet he grabbed the camp-stool and pursued the Man from New Hampshire around the corner of the tent, followed by our volleying laughter, while even the Indians standing around grinned broadly.

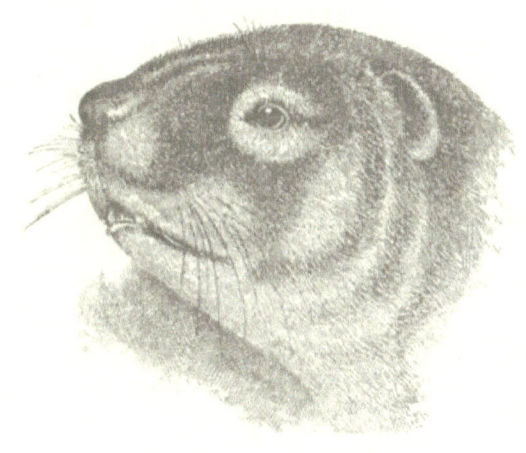

CHAPTER IX.

A STRANGE MIDNIGHT RIDE.

>   Is there not
> A tongue in every star, that talks with man,
> And wooes him to be wise ? Nor wooes in vain.
> This dead of midnight is the noon of thought,
> And wisdom mounts her zenith with the stars.

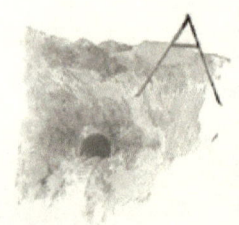A RIDE, — and such a ride as no ancient ever took, although he were a god; a ride upon a steed without feet or wings, and yet a steed which swept us through sunlit space and starlit gloom faster than hoof of speed or flight of wing. To the south, the prairie land stretched green and fragrant with summer growth and bloom to the far southern Gulf. To the north, the same lovely level swept to the lower edge of the great Mackenzie basin, — that far river of the north of which few know but little, and most know nothing. Its length, longer than the Mississippi's; its climate, although upon the edge and within the rim of the Arctic circle, still warmer than Dakota's; its plains, within whose vast

boundaries Eastern States and Provinces might be placed and lost; the growth of its rich soils, barley, wheat, peas, and all life-feeding vegetables, together with those hardy flowers which grace our Northern tables: these and other marvels born of isothermal lines which, curving hither and yon, laugh at lines of latitude, — are not these things scoffed at by the stay-at-homes as myths and idle tales? Why, then, tell of the great possibilities for healthy men and happy homes lying far to the north of present settlements; of millions on millions of acres that only wait for the plough and the seed, the sower's hand and the harvester's sickle, to yield the hungry world the bread it needs, if it will not believe the truth? Yet the world will read the poetry of this far-stretching land, and, reading it, will by and by come to the knowledge of its economic facts, — perhaps.

To the south, then, the plains stretched to the Gulf; to the north, half as far. To the east, the great lawn extended nigh three hundred leagues. To the west, in the glory of sunset, its sapphire splendors spread over the fixed blue of heaven and the floating fleece of clouds, arose the barrier of a great mountain wall which reached to the south and north as far as eye might see. Never in all my journeyings had I seen such a sight. The foothills, in the distance and gathering gloom, were flattened out of view, and the green prairie land spread to the very foot of that majestic wall, as level as a floor. At the far edge of this extended emerald field, the monstrous range, its hither side darkened with firs and evening's gloom, rose in might and ma-

CAÑON OF THE THOMPSON.

jesty. It was as if I had come at last to the very edge of the world, which God had fenced and barricaded, fixing with almighty power the limit of man's wandering and discoveries.

Toward this monstrous barricade, this base of gloom that stretched far as the eye might see to the north and south, we drove in silence. Behind this wall the red sun slowly sank. I saw its quivering orb of flame rest on a peak of snow that at its touch kindled to the brightness of a burning star. On either hand a hundred other peaks flashed like newly lighted beacons. Is it for warning or for guidance, I queried to myself, — for the weird sight stirred my imagination unwontedly, — that those hundred beacon fires, stretching in front of me on either hand a hundred miles, are kindled high in heaven?

Thus, then, was I hurried onward fast as set wings might carry me, with my gaze on the peaks, the fading fire in the sky, and the growing gloom. Slowly the crimson faded; slowly the sapphire colors lost their splendors; slowly the orange lights were blanched, and the warm tones that filled the heavens chilled into gray, and then in the far distance my eye saw only a blue sky pointed here and there with starry fire, and between it and me, sharply edged, cleanly cut, strongly defined, stood forth domes of snow and pinnacles of ice.

Many sights of splendor have I seen in wandering by day and night; many pictures such as man's hand could never paint have I gazed at, both at noontide and at midnight, when for my entertainment, as it seemed,

— for being there alone I only saw, — Nature kindly shifted her etched or painted scrolls. Many weird sights have I gazed at floating on northern waters in the night time, when all the woods were silent with local stillness, and round the Pole, by hands unnamed by science, unknown to superstition even, were lighted the mystic fires which illuminate with awful and shifting splendors the end of the world. But never in wandering by day or night, on plain or mountain slope, or surface of forest lakes, have my eyes beheld a spectacle so strange and startling, or an exhibition so magnificent, as I saw, gazing westward through the gloom at the summits of the Rocky Mountains, with the world around me darkened into gloaming and the dead sunset lying on the bier of Night beyond. Between the dark earth and the blue sky, the black flatness and the star-lighted dome, the whiteness of the peaks drew a line of startling effects from north to south, held in mysterious suspension between earth and heaven as far as eye might range.

Steadily we rolled onward. Behind, the roar and rumble of the train; ahead, the stillness of nature's undisturbed repose when man sleeps and animals walk velvet-footed. The sun had set. The moon had not risen; yet it was not dark. A strange half-light filled the world. The train I could not see, for I was riding ahead of it. The power that drew it, whose mighty throbbings I could feel as though within me, pushed me through the air as an arrow is pushed from the bow. I was being whirled along as a bird is whirled when it rides the tempest. The dusk was fragrant with unseen bloom. The earth odors were blown into my nostrils. I breathed the strong life of the world, and felt its strength come to me as I breathed.

Suddenly, on my left, I saw a snowy owl sailing with set wings westward. Was it the ghost of the day that had just died that had been forced at last to leave the world it loved so well? The spectral vision raced us a race and won, and far ahead I saw its snowy plumage fade and lose itself in the distance. A flock of ducks, startled from the sedges of the lake we skirted, whirred upward out of sight. I thought it strange that I could hear their feathered stroke so far away. Above me the great round eye of the headlight blazed like a sun. A coyote sprang upon the track, stood for a moment gazing at us, its eyes two diamond sparks, its dirty gray coat gleaming white and beautiful as silk, then slunk away, and the gloaming hid it from sight. Suddenly, above us and ahead, a flock of mighty birds swept into view, — their bodies white, their legs half the length of a man's, their long, broad bills crooked like a spoon, yellow as gold, their wings, shading from their white bodies into raven black, stretched wider than a man's hands could reach. They were pelicans, those mighty birds that float upon the prairie lakes as large as swans, whose vans beat the air with strokes stronger than an eagle's. One such bird might make a trophy for a hunter more noble than horns of elk or head of moose. They gave no cry, but circled like spectres into sight, and like a ghostly visitation disappeared. Thus into the night I glided, holding converse with the night, — a wingless bird myself, flying with birds.

Those who know Nature only by day know only half of her, and the least interesting half at that. Nature has two faces. Both are beautiful, but one is supremely so. The one is as a human face, glowing, sunlighted, tanned, scarred, it may be, perfect or imperfect, as the day is. Her night-time face is as an angel's, the face of one that has been translated from flesh to spirit, and by the translation lost its grossness and become etherealized. Its beauty is that beauty which is veiled, which gains from having its loveliness suggested rather than revealed. The nude is always unsatisfactory, for loveliness is ever a thing of suggestion rather than revelation. He who sees all plainly sees too much. As sight would rob religion of the glory of faith, so it robs loveliness of the benefits of imagination.

One may tire of Nature by day, — the sun makes her common. When morning has fully come, we may go within-doors and eat; we may go to our toil; we may strike our tents and move on, weary of the dusty road. For not until the glare is passed and the hot sun dimmed by coming shadows and cooled by falling dew, need we halt on the march or come forth from our doors to look about us. Verily to the lover of Nature, whether on plain or amid hills, or shore of sea, the night is the time to wake. Then should eyes be opened as stars and orbed for vision, as is the moon when it rolls in rounded perfection through the lighted skies.

And oh, the voices of the night! The day is tuneless. Man monopolizes it with his noises; with the murmurs of his trade, the roar and rumble of his commerce; with the strident calls of his shoutings, his cursing, and his turbulence. But with the night comes that silence which is vocal. Then Nature sings. Her tunefulness is heard abroad, and her soft melodies come sweetly to listening ears. The sod finds speech; the brook murmurs to the banks; the trees whisper and call in sylvan concert; and through all the fields a thousand tongues, unknown among the languages of men, break forth in sweet expression.

To many I know that what I write will be a mystery, or only as the joining of meaningless words, but to others it will come freighted with soberness and truth. For they, as well as I, have camped upon the shores of lakes amid the circling woods; have stood alone at night on boundless prairies, and thrown themselves down amid the grasses and flowers, unable to sleep because of the glory that was above them, the odors that they breathed, and the sweet sounds which came to their charmed ears from nigh or far. And others yet have stood upon the top of mountains when the sun went down, and with gladness seen the shadows darken and the stars come out, watching for them as for loved faces not seen for years, and have sat on the bare rocks, hour after hour, and watched them draw their golden circles through the blue above, and in the silence heard all the tones of memory and the prophecies of hope. And when at last they slept they found the granite softer than a downy bed shut in with walls and doors. These, reading, know what I mean, and that I say the truth and lie not when I say that he who has seen Nature only by day has seen only the lesser half of her, and in one sense, and a true one too, has not seen her at all.

Still onward we drove. Here and there the grade sloped downward, and then the mighty train flew like a  meteor. It was not riding; we were being projected into space, we were being shot through the air. The atmosphere was cool, dewy, fragrant. In the declensions of the prairie, fields of white fog enveloped the track. Into and through these soft layers of fleece our faces dashed. Out of them they rose as from a bath of spray, dripping with perfumed water. How delicious the sense of life became! There was not a slow vein in us. We flowed full to the brim with vitality. The consciousness of happy, buoyant life was in us as never before. The wild forces of the world were round us, and we were of them. We were of the atoms of the universe, of which each atom is superlatively vital. We were all alive. We throbbed and panted on the rising grades like the engine. Down the long declensions we reeled and rollicked like a frolicsome meteor. We whirled along through the gloom like the birds of night which we startled from the sedges. We rolled billowing onward like the great herds of cattle which our shrieking flight stampeded. We thundered around the bends of the river furiously, and the snorting horses in mighty bands burst wildly away from the blaze of our headlight as we dashed into the ranches, heads tossing from side to side, eyes blazing like diamonds, manes and tails streaming their pomp and pride of flowing hair afar.

Thus through the short summer night we rode or flew. Twice the monster that bore us so steadily and swiftly stopped at water and stood panting. Around it crowded a mob of wild-looking creatures,— the Indians of the plains; Blackfeet, who rank with the Sioux for courage; Crees, whose kindred wigwams stretched to the coast of Labrador; the Assinniboins or "Stonies," whose tongue connects them dimly with the tribes which trap upon the shores of far Mistassinni; these and the scattered remnants of other tribes thronged around, wrapped within blankets, silently gazing at us as we sat upon the engine. A wilder-looking set of beings no man ever saw. Their long, coarse, raven-black hair hung low upon their bosoms and shoulders. The wind at times blew the black tangle of it over their faces. These were painted with red and yellow ochres, which heightened indescribably their wild, fierce aspect. Their blankets were of high colors, some of a solid red, some red with black stripes, while others were checkered in blazing squares. The plumes of eagle, raven, and pelican were knotted in their coarse locks. They said nothing. They asked no alms. The brakemen, oilers, and wheel-testers flashed their lanterns into their faces, and joked them pleasantly. They made no answer and they never stirred. What were their thoughts? I will stir them up, I said.

I stepped to the side of an old chief, — a tall, wrinkled, and withered Blackfoot, — and said, "Chief, are you thinking that this prairie land was the land of your fathers for a thousand years? that their bones are under its flowers to-night, and that their spirits are hunting the deer and the buffalo this minute on the mighty sand-hills there to the east? that this fiery monster I am riding is the Evil Power that has banished your game, robbed you of your hunting-grounds, and destroyed the strength and glory of your race? Do you not hate it and us who manage and use it?" He listened with his gaze full on me. I knew by the flash that came into the black eyes that he understood, but his face gave no sign and he spake not a word. But I had told him the truth, and he knew it.

The Indians you meet on the line of this Canadian

SAPOMAXICOW, OR CROWFOOT,

Chief of the Black Feet Indians.

road are finer specimens of the red race than those met with on the lines that run through the States. The early French treated the Indians with humanity, the English with barbarity. The Hudson's Bay Company's commercial instincts prompted wisdom, — the wisdom of justice and mercy; and so its factors and agents continued on in the line of humane French precedence. The Canadian government naturally fell heir to this policy of wisdom, and in the main has striven honestly to live up to it. The beneficial effect of this treatment is apparent to the most casual observer. The Indians of the Canadian west and northwest are not like the debauched and degraded vagabonds we find hanging around the stations of our Western railroads. They are well-clothed, cleanly, healthy-looking, and in many cases fine specimens of the red race. The women are well dressed and of decent appearance. The boys look vigorous and the girls healthy, and not a few of them handsome. They look as if they were still capable of taking care of themselves, still had a right to live, and a place reserved for them by the bond of honorable engagement in the land of their fathers. Instead of being a painful spectacle to the Continental tourist, the Indians of the plains between Winnipeg and the Rocky Mountains, a stretch of nearly a thousand miles, are objects of interest and pleasant surprise.

At last we noticed a change in the air ahead of us. The darkness began to change to gray. The stars above us shone with shorter beams. A pale light spread over the vast plain. A flock of geese wedged their way laboriously northward through the ashen gloom. To the left, in the bend of Bow River, a herd of cattle stood in the fog, their heads and backs showing above the white fleece, their bodies invisible — a strange effect. The old, old fight, older than the world, was being waged around us, — the fight of light with darkness. The attack and defence were equally stubborn. There were no charges, no sudden dashes, no quick recoil or recoveries of position. The movements were vast, slow-motioned, immense. The stars from pole to pole telegraphed the result. The horizon line of the whole world showed us, as we gazed, the victory and the defeat. Suddenly, high in heaven, the summits of the mountains, an endless line, shone pearly white. Below the gleaming spires their monstrous bulks were black as night. It was a sight to see with lifted hands. Then all the world grew rosy. The low-lying fog fields crimsoned. The foothills sprang into view. The clouds blushed. The sun without warning had kissed them. The icy peaks flashed white like electric lights. The sun leaped from the far eastern grasses, and Morning, with a rush of glorious color on her face, took vivid possession of the world. And thus, with faces wet with dew, our nostrils filled with forest odors, our eyes bright as the eyes of those who had discovered a new world, we dashed into the amphitheatre of the everlasting hills, and stopped at last, our glorious ride ended, and stood, in the red light of the morning, gazing bewildered, astonished, at that marvellous expression of Nature's beauty and majesty known to the tourist of this western world as *Banff*.

CHAPTER X.

BANFF.

"There was a sound of revelry by night."

"ON the northeast side of Scotland, if you will look at your maps, gentlemen," said the Judge, "you will find this name of Banff. To tell you the story of its transplanting would be to give you the history of a life, — a life which began there, and being removed here developed into one of the strongest personalities of the continent. The once poor boy at Banff has since become one of the chief forces of this western world. No higher compliment could be paid him than to give this magnificent location the name of his birthplace. But no one who knows the modesty and greatness of the man, and the services he has done this country, will say that the compliment is excessive."

"There is no reward too great," exclaimed Mr. Pepperell, "there is no reward too great for a man whose faith and courage have opened up such a country as this to civilization. Such a man has enlarged the opportunity of human effort, and made happy and prosperous homes possible to millions."

We were standing at the celebrated Sulphur Spring at the time, one of the many natural curiosities which make this location famous. There were only four of us left, — the Judge, Mr. Pepperell, the Man from New Hampshire, and myself. We were all old travellers, and saw that in Banff alone we had a good week's entertainment, without going beyond it a rod.

"This water smells bad enough to cure a man, that is, if he was very sick," said the New Hampshire man quietly, as he lifted a cup of the heavily-tinctured water to his nose.

"I know a man who left his lameness in that spring," said the Judge, reflectively.

"It may be that is what I smell," added the Man from New Hampshire, laconically.

By this time we had passed through the tunnel that has been bored into the ledge, in the centre of which Nature had hollowed that strange cavern from whose bottom boil the waters of healing.

"At that time," continued the Judge, ignoring as not worthy his attention the facetious remark of our companion, "at that time, this passage had not been excavated, and the only way to reach this curative pool was to be lowered by a rope through that aperture, up there," and he pointed to the hole at the centre of the cavern's dome, some two feet in diameter, through which we could see the sky, and which originally gave vent to the heated atmosphere of the warm spring within.

"They say," said Mr. Pepperell, "that the Indians used to bring their sick to this mountain side, and lower them through that hole into the warm sulphurous water; and they declare that not a single man ever spent a day and a night in this cavern that was n't lifted out well."

"It would n't have taken a day and a night to have cured me," said the Man from New Hampshire, as he stopped his nose and started for the tunnel. "Any man would be a fool not to swear he was cured after being ten minutes in this oven; for before this passage was cut, which gives its chimney a draft, it must have been close, mighty close, in here!"

"It does n't smell like a rose," laughingly returned the Judge, as he shuffled on after us, "but a man will stand sulphur pretty strong to get rid of rheumatism."

"They say that this whole mountain has a substratum of sulphur," remarked Mr. Pepperell, after he had taken two or three whiffs of pure air, beyond the mouth of the passage.

"The Indians are poor theologians," said the Man from New Hampshire. "They located their hell at the Glacier; they should have brought it this side of the range."

"I have always thought it strange," remarked the Judge, "that a man with the knowledge of Milton should have connected sulphur with the punitive suffering of the race, when, in fact, it is one of the most potent of all curative principles."

"Perfectly adapted for Purgatory," quietly remarked the Man from New Hampshire.

I presume that four men never enjoyed a happier week than we spent at Banff. We rolled leisurely over the fine roads that the government had constructed, winding in and out along the bends of the Bow River, running along the base of the gigantic mountains and through the cool forests of the firs. We explored, with the curiosity and eagerness of boys, the secluded places, and followed the dim by-paths, not knowing or caring whither they led us, happy, whether they conducted us to some noble prospect or terminated suddenly at some dripping ledge. We searched for curious minerals in the sides of the mountains, translated the geological records of the cliffs, and collected polished pebbles from the bed of the foaming Spray. We slept at noonday under the pines, lulled to sleep by the Falls of the Bow, and fished, not in vain, for its noted trout in the rapids. We watched the storm clouds vainly assault the monstrous mountains, that lifted their heads majestically above the reach of storms; listened to the thunder as it bellowed in the gorges and rumbled down the ravines; saw the rainbows grow, and shrink their arches of splendor, and fade away; and, at evening, sat in the great angle of the veranda which overlooked the Falls five hundred

THE BOW RIVER, BANFF.

feet below us, and saw the round moon roll up above the Fairholme range, and whiten the valley of the Bow with its silvery light. We admired the ample design of the commodious house, — a veritable palace, with interior finish of native woods polished to a gleam; its wide stairways and galleries; the noble dining-room, with its lofty ceiling, which the Judge pronounced " fit to be a banquet-hall for the gods; " and the large verandas that encircled the entire house, as if to invite the guest to enjoy, to their fill, the majestic scenery which stood grouped around it.

"Here," exclaimed Mr. Bonneville, "here, is a continental enterprise of which, as a continental man, I am proud. A year ago and what was there here? A forest, a solitude. And out of that forest and solitude, at the touch of courageous enterprise, this noble structure has risen with all its appurtenances of comfort and luxury, as in the mind of the dreamer a vision arises in the darkness of night."

"The only vision," said the Man from New Hampshire, "that while it delights the eye, ever fully satisfied the stomach."

"The climax of civilization," remarked the Judge contentedly, as he accepted a cigar from Mr. Pepperell's case. "A perfect climax of civilization. The dessert at dinner to-day made me profoundly grateful that I was not born a barbarian."

"Had you been, you would have civilized the tribe and imported a French *chef*, Judge," retorted the New Hampshire man laughingly.

At the appointed day the scattered members of the

party kept their rendezvous at the hotel. The house swarmed with guests. A cosmopolitan company in truth. The continent in its every section, almost, was represented. The nations of Europe and the islands of the seas were there. The flags of old England, of France, and of the Great Republic were fraternally intertwined. Science and art, poetry and letters, music, beauty, and wit were joined in bright companionship. A programme for the evening's entertainment had been prepared and the Judge appointed master of ceremonies. The stars lighted the world outside, and within the electric globes flooded the house with their white radiance.

"Ladies and gentlemen," began the Judge, "this is not, I will honestly confess, my maiden speech, and yet I find myself affected as if it were. I am embarrassed, not at the courtesy of your suffrage, but at the novelty of my position. A citizen of the Golden Gate, I find myself in the Dominion of the Queen, surrounded by an audience representing almost every section of that Empire on which the sun never sets, every State and Territory of the Great Republic, and almost every civilized nation on the face of the earth. We, the citizens of the Republic, moved by love of country and of institutions which are precious to every lover of liberty wherever he is found, wish to hold a social reunion. With that modesty for which we Americans are noted the world around, we proceeded promptly to appropriate this hotel and all the resources for entertainment in the establishment, including yourselves, surreptitiously inveigled under the name of guests, that

MT. STEPHEN.

your elegance, your wit, and your beauty might add *éclat* to the occasion. This piratical proceeding we proceeded to legalize by a process invented by us Yankees known as the 'Town Meeting;' a process which has been wittily described as enabling the original New Englander to steal his lands from the Indians, become a rebel to his king, and change the commandments without doing violence to his conscience. At this meeting of my fellow-countrymen I was elected master of ceremonies, a dignity which I did not obtain, according to a quaint national custom prevalent among us, without being openly charged by my competitors with having reached the lofty elevation by a scandalous stuffing of the ballot-box. Here amid these everlasting hills, in this palace of modern luxury, with the flags of all nations intertwined, emblematic of that peace which not only now prevails in the Republic and its relations, but through the Empire of the English-speaking race, and with an audience more truly cosmopolitan than I have ever seen outside of the official halls of government, we hold our happy reunion. We Americans are not formal. We are not exclusive. The liberties of refinement will rule the evening. Literature will be honored. Music will be applauded. Beauty will be admired, genius receive its acclaim, the banquet table be spread, and then Terpsichore shall dance to the music of the hours, till the flush of morning shall turn the icy pinnacles of the mountains above us to the color of the rose."

There was just that Fourth of July swing to the eloquence of the Judge, that rhetorical abandon, which suited exactly the mood of his fellow-countrymen, and we all cheered him as none of us have ever been cheered since our Class Day oration, when we electrified our sisters, our cousins, and our aunts with the flights of our eloquence. We all cheered him immensely. The Man from New Hampshire, who had been a self-nominated rival to the Judge in his struggle for the chairmanship, prolonged his applause as if, like a true American when defeated, he would triumph over his hated rival by the exhibition of his generosity.

"Ladies and gentlemen," resumed the Judge, when the Man from New Hampshire had subsided, feeling that he was the true victor, "ladies and gentlemen, I will first present to you Professor Blankton, of the Continental College, an Institution not yet erected, but which nevertheless stands completed to the eye of faith, on the subscription paper — not largely subscribed to as yet — which he carries in his pocket. Professor Blankton will give us a recitation of an original composition prepared expressly for this occasion, called The Two Flags."

"That you may understand, ladies and gentlemen," began the Professor, as with a graceful bow he acknowledged the generous reception we gave him, "that you may understand the location and natural surroundings of this little episode of American-Canadian life, which I am to render, I will briefly describe them to you.

"Below the Fraser Cañon, the savage sublimity of which cannot perhaps be equaled on the continent, the

Fraser curves to the right, and sends its deep, strong, down-rushing current with a sullen roar against the base of a mountain. And he who stands in the curve below Yale, and looks up that wide reach of water to where it rushes out of the gloomy pass, from between walls of rocks which rise six thousand feet above it, sees as grand a spectacle and as sublime a vision of river and mountain as he may find on the continent. Opposite this curve, on which you will imagine yourself standing, stretches a plain, acres in extent, lying enclosed in the curve of the great stream, under the rounded banks of which, when the water is lowest in summer, stretches a bar of brown sand. From that bar a crowd of Americans, who had broken through the vast mountains from California, in 1868, took in a few days more than a million of dollars of granulated gold. From this fact it received the name of American Bar, a name which it retains to this day. On the plain above the bar, directly in front of the monstrous mouth of the Fraser Cañon, were camped more than six hundred of our fellow-countrymen.

"It is doubtful, ladies and gentlemen, if a rougher, braver, more reckless crowd were ever seen in British Columbia. They represented the frontier of our country; that frontier which stands for exploration, mad ventures, audacious enterprises, personal courage, coarse bravado, manhood wrecked, recklessness of life, and generous impulses. In it, every State and Territory of the Union had its spokesman. The dialect, the personal characteristics, the humor, even the profanity of each section was represented by its true type. Many were old forty-niners, men who had crossed the plains on foot, rifle in hand, when the East went wild at the news that gold could be had for the digging beyond the Nevadas. Youth and age and middle life were there. Ex-army men, Blue and Gray, Reb and Yank, worked as partners, and starved, feasted, or gambled together as luck smiled or frowned. Some signed their name with that sign which stands with equal facility for piety or ignorance; and others in the hush of evening sang the songs of their Alma Mater to the listening pines and silent stars. Many were ignorant of any grammar, and others might have served as Queen's Messengers, not only in European but in Asiatic courts. Many were scarred with wounds received in battle or private fights. All were armed, and ate and slept with a pistol at their hips. And while they gambled or bet heavily when in money or liquor, nevertheless drunkenness was exceptional and fights uncommon. A crude but effectively administered justice guarded property and life. Thieving was unknown at American Bar. 'It does n't pay,' said Light-fingered Dick to his partner, who had learned a useful trade under the direction of his native State: 'it does n't pay in a community so damned ignorant that the court has only one classification for crimes and inflicts but one penalty.' Still it cannot be said that this crowd of gold-seekers were precisely the kind of men one would select for church-membership, and certainly more reckless dare-deviltry was camped that summer at American Bar than could be easily grouped in any other spot on the face of the earth. You now

FRASER CAÑON, BELOW NORTH BEND.

have the knowledge of the location and characteristics of the occurrence, and I will proceed to give you the story of —

THE TWO FLAGS.

"Let these two flags go on like twin
Stars in equal courses moving."

"It was the Fourth of July. The sun stood equidistant between the monstrous cliffs that made the walls of the Black Cañon, pouring its rays straight downward upon the foam-whitened surface of the racing water. On the plain in the elbow of the river stood the camp, and on the bush-cabins and old, soiled tents the rays fell brightly and hot; all the hotter they seemed to the revelers on the sand, because above and around them, as they looked through the heated air, they could see the cold gleam of glaciers and the glint of ice against the blue sky. The camp was in holiday mood; not a man was at work at the Bar. To have lifted pick or pan would have started Judge Lynch that day. They had struck luck at the Bar and their mood was exuberant. Some were pitching quoits, using small bags of gold dust for their quoits, each caster risking the bag that he cast; others were engaged in pistol practice, the bull's-eye being a gold eagle at fifty yards. The bullet that hit won the eagle. Some were whirling knives at bank notes. In every tent poker was being played with a recklessness that would frighten a railroad magnate. Two men were pronouncing an oration on Liberty at either end of the camp, while a scholarly looking man, considerably exhilarated with something stronger than the inspiration of the poet, was vainly endeavoring to pronounce the measures of a patriotic ode he had composed to a throng of uproarious auditors.

"Suddenly at the mountain end of the central street, a throng of men appeared, bearing on their shoulders a flag-staff with the halyards all rigged. At their head marched Hoosier Jack, who was 'loaded with lead' at Shiloh, carrying a staff from which waved a yard of bunting, with its thirteen stars all faded and the glorious stripes sadly bleached, frayed at the edges, if the truth must be told, and 'damnably out of repairs,' as Bangor Harry asserted; but symbolic still of liberty to man, and of the great country which stands for that liberty the world over. Ahead of it marched the band, composed of a little snare drum, two fifes, and five fiddles, playing Yankee Doodle with a celerity of movement and an earnestness of expression which more than compensated for the artistic deficiencies of the performance.

"But, oh! the cheers and the yells that greeted that little cheap flag as it came down the street! The emptying of tents, the rushing of the gamblers; the pell-mell that ensued! In the rear of those bearing the flag-staff the procession was formed, and twice through the camp the cheap, faded banner was carried, and then in the centre the flag-pole was set, the bunting knotted to the halyards, and up went the Stars and Stripes, while every head was uncovered and the eyes of many grew dim as they gazed. And as the flag went up and the breeze shook it out and the sunshine brightened the faded stars and bleached stripes, a cheer, hoarse and strong, stormed upward like the roar of a tempest, startling the goats on the crag and the fish-hawks at the mouth of the Cañon, and Bangor Harry, climbing to the top of some cracker-boxes with his six shooter for his baton, constituted himself leader of the music of the occasion, and in his clear tenor voice, resonant as a bugler's call at sunrise, began, —

> 'Yes, we'll rally round the flag, boys,
>   We'll rally once again,
> Shouting the battle-cry of Freedom;
>   We'll rally from the hillside,
>   We'll gather from the plain,
> Shouting the battle-cry of Freedom.
> *Chorus:* The Union forever!
>   Hurrah! boys, hurrah!
>   Down with the traitor, up with the star,
> While we rally round the flag, boys,
>   Rally once again,
> Shouting the battle-cry of Freedom.'

"Whether it was the exhilaration of the occasion, the swing and sweep of the verse, or the thrill of pride that the symbol above their heads was theirs once more, or the magical memories of the old days before the war, we cannot say, but we simply record the fact that when the singer had reached the chorus, and the great crowd of rough, bronzed, strong men took up the refrain, Arkansas Reb and Mississippi Pete, who had 'bored the old flag' in twenty battles, joined in as vigorously as if they had been born under the slope of Bunker Hill.

"The song closed in a roar of sound which might not be designated by Thomas or Zerrahn as music, but which fully answered the demands of the occasion, and at a word from Bangor Harry, every revolver left its owner's hip, and six hundred polished muzzles gleamed in the sun. Six volleys followed the signal of the leader with a precision which demonstrated that they were more practiced in the use of the "iron" than in the chromatic scale.

"'You fellows,' said Bangor Harry, as he crawled carefully down from the top of his cracker-boxes, 'you fellows ain't much at singing, but you have all got the classical touch on the trigger.'

"It was in fact an exuberant and exciting crowd, a crowd which the least touch would have exploded for fun, patriotism, or deviltry. And it was at this unfortunate juncture — unfortunate for him — that out of his bush shanty crawled Bloody Edwards, a big, aggressive, red-faced London cockney, who had come through the mountains with the crowd from no imaginable reason save sheer accident, and still remained with them because of tolerance on their part and excessive indolence on his; for there certainly was nothing in common between this lofty-acting, boastful cockney from London and the free and easy, reckless men among whom he was staying. A more boastful, swaggering braggart never breathed. The most offensive Briton was in him typed most offensively. His favorite superlative was 'bloody!' It answered even the purpose of his loyalty, which was so excessive as to tax language to express, and gave him his name.

"At the very moment when the vast crowd was fairly boiling over with excitement and ready for any mischief, came Bloody Edwards upon the scene, swaggering offensively and waving a small, red, British flag in his hand. Planting himself in the centre of the street in front of the six hundred exhilarated Americans, he waved the little banner flauntingly over his head, and howled —

"'Urrah for the Flag of Hold Hingland!'

"For an instant the crowd never moved; each man stood silently in his tracks, and then with a roar came the rush. It struck Bloody Edwards like a land slide, and swept him, as if he were a bit of *débris*, to the bank of the river. Then out of the roar lanced a voice, 'Naturalize him! naturalize him! Make a Yankee out of the cockney!' and six hundred voices took up the cry — for the humor of the idea pleased them — 'Aye, aye! Naturalize him; he shall take the oath of allegiance. Make him swear by the Stars and Stripes!'

"But the cockney refused to become a Yankee; refused point blank, and garnished his refusal by expletives known only to the slums of London.

"'Curse the cockney,' exclaimed Cambridge Jack, 'the fool acts as if he had a choice in the matter;' and then he screamed, 'Dip him! Dip him! Cool him down in the Fraser! He shall swear by the Stars and Stripes, or drown!' And the crowd took up the words of Cambridge Jack, for the cockney had no friends; he had not acted to make any, and surely no flag up to this time had ever had a less manly representative than the banner of England had found in the person of this boasting, swaggering, insolent cockney, Bloody Edwards. And so the crowd took up the cry of Cambridge Jack, prompted thereto by the sense of humor and the dislike of the cockney, and yelled, 'Into the Fraser with him! Cool him down! Teach him manners! He shall swear by the Stars and Stripes, or drown!' And then the crowd gave one surge, and upward the cockney was swung, and down to the river they rushed him, and into the depth of the cold, icy river, that river that never was warm and never will warm until the elements melt, they plunged him.

"But underneath and within the punk of his cockneyism, untouched by the rot of the surface, was a sound streak of old English oak. For as the big, red face came out of the ice-cold tide, he blew like a porpoise and yelled again, —

"'Urrah for the flag of Hold Hingland!'

"'Down with him! Down with him again!' yelled the crowd to Blarney Pat and Confederate Dick who had him in hand. And downward they plunged him; down into the coldness of death, that glacial cold in that river of glaciers which chills and whitens quick and sure for the grave. Downward they sent him and again, as he came to the surface, he feebly sputtered, —

"'Urrah — for — the — flag — of — Hold — Hin — gland!'

"By this time it was evident that Bloody Edwards was sober, sober as a man who from birthday had never touched ale, and that it was not the reckless bravado born of liquor, but the bull-dog grit which made

Poictiers, Cressy, and Waterloo what they stand for, which held him to the line whose ghastly white men dread, so stiffly — the indomitable English grit that was in him.

"And this it was which won on the crowd and even on the two men who had twice plunged him into that death-cold current, that current which never yet gave back to light of day a body that once touched its bottom. For Confederate Dick, as he looked into the big, red English face that now lay drooping weakly on the bull-like neck, exclaimed in sheer disgust, —

"'Curse the English fool, he won't give in!' Then up spoke Bangor Harry, as he thrust himself to the front of the surging crowd.

"'Boys, the darned fool is of the same blood with us if he is beefy built; for his grit proves it. The red flag he'd die for owned the continent before the Stars and Stripes split it. And the two own the continent still betwixt them, and shall own it forever, by Heaven! Three cheers for the red flag of England, the old mother-land of us all.' And suddenly out of the throats of the six hundred men who had swarmed over the border searching for gold, above whose heads floated the little, cheap fifteen by twenty bunting with its stars bleached and its stripes all faded, there burst as hearty a cheer for the cross of St. George as ever English gunners sent from bloody English decks when through the smoke they saw their foeman's flag come floating down.

"Then out of the water they lifted the cockney, they rolled him and rubbed him, and twenty flasks were tossed through the air to the men who had him in hand. Then they took the flag, — Cambridge Jack was the man, — and bent it to the halyards, side by side with the Stars and Stripes, and they hoisted the two with loud cheers.

"'Divil take the rag!' said Blarney Pat as he pulled lustily away at the halyards. 'Divil take the rag, but the b'y that won Waterloo was born nigh Killarney!'

"But this was not all, for a strange thing happened, strange enough at any time, but doubly so happening at that very moment. Scarcely had the cheering died than along the river's farther bank there came a circling wind, marking its progress with dust, dead leaves, and withered grasses, which at its touch sprang upward into air. Across the rushing river, across the Bar, it ran its circling course, jumped the dry bank and rushed across the bend, and in its career struck full and fair the staff from which the kindred banners waved; out of their fastenings tore them, and, twined together, blent as one, sent them soaring upward through the sunshine toward the blue sky and the white summits of the Cañon, eight thousand feet above the throng of swarthy, scarred, and startled faces gazing at them.

"Thus in silence stood the camp. Not a sound was heard save the rush of water as it whirled around the Bar or fretted along the shifting edges of the golden beach below. Spellbound and marveling at such strange hap, their jests all checked, their rude talk silenced, they stood at gaze, their eyes fixed on the flags as they went up and onward, lifted higher and higher into the blue. Still upward and onward they soared; and not until they were to the eye but a fleck of color, not until that fleck of color had touched the level of the icy peaks and the summit line of snow, not until the winds which pour forever over them had caught the flags and they were about to disappear, borne on by winds which flow forever round the world, was that solemn silence broken. But as the blended flags, now but a speck of color, were about to fade forever from their gazing eyes, the voice of Bangor Harry rose strong and clear, with the genuine Yankee nasal struck clean through the words: —

"'*I'll be darned if God Almighty has n't joined them two flags together!*'"

The Man from New Hampshire was mightily stirred by the recitation, and when he lifted himself from his chair, and standing erect, swung his white beaver over his head and cried, "Hurrah for the flag of Old England, the mother-land of us all!" the great veranda trembled to the roar of the applause which burst from the laughing, cheering throng.

Then

"Music arose with its voluptuous swell.
  Soft eyes looked love to eyes that spake again,
And all went merry as a marriage bell."

The long, wide piazzas made such an ideal ball-room as is seldom seen

"When youth and pleasure meet
  To chase the glowing hours with flying feet,"

for above them the blue star-fretted heaven was for a roof, and the free, odor-filled breeze of the mountains gave to the waltzers such air as eagles breathe. Beneath their feet the polished floor, under the electric lights, shone like ground of glass; upon the hills and into the valley the moon poured its soft light, while to the music of the band the Falls far below added its steady roar — a heavy monotone of power softened by distance. Into the solemn solitude of nature, into the undisturbed silence of ages, within the enclosure of mountains old as the world, whose summits were white with snow that fell in the morning of Time and had never melted, man — the social man — had burst, erected his palace, spread a table of banquet, and summoned music and pleasure to the feast. The strength and grace of form, the gleam of silks, the flow of soft-toned draperies, the flash of gems, the loveliness of snowy necks and arms, the glowing cheek, the laughing lip, the buzz of happy talk, the harmonies of music — all were here, making a rare, sweet, bright picture of human happiness. So passed the hours until the dawn gave rosy signal for retiring and the first "American Night" at Banff ended, as it should, in a lovely morning.

ON THE TOTE ROAD.

CHAPTER XI.

NAMELESS MOUNTAINS.

" Hills piled on hills, on mountains mountains lie."

FROM the Gap, but a little way beyond the beautiful Kananaskis Falls, to Yale at the outlet of the celebrated Fraser Cañon is nearly five hundred miles, and it is a very moderate statement to say that nowhere else on this continent or in Europe can the tourist see from his parlor car such a magnificent exhibition of mountain scenery. Here is a section of the transcontinental journey in respect to which the traveler can experience no disappointment. It is not only that he is constantly running along the base of mountains of gigantic size and immense altitude by which he is stimulated and impressed, but these mountains are of every shape and color, present themselves to the eye in an infinite variety of appearance, and are individualized by strong, novel, and imposing characteristics. Here stands one of such immense bulk and height, holding such a relation to the line of travel, that it dominates the landscape and fills the gazer's horizon from edge to edge. Passing this monstrous obstruction to the vision, the eye suddenly beholds a range pinnacled with eternal snow and flashing crests of ice, whose brilliancy is the reflection of ages. Anon, he is whirled around a curve, on a track so cut into the beetling cliffs that at a distance it looks like a dark thread spun in the air and drifted by the wind against the perpendicular wall, and lo, he is in the midst of a hundred mountains, tumbled promiscuously together, a vast jumble of chaotic misplacement. At one moment he is rolling swiftly down a valley, as green with springing verdure, as odorous with flowers, as peaceful and lonely, as the Happy Valley of Rasselas; above it the bluest of skies and the brightest of suns, with a flashing river running with musical ripplings through its centre; and at the next, the train is groping its way along a narrow gorge cut sheer through a mountain range at the level of its base, with the black, rocky sides rising abruptly thousands of feet on either hand, a river of vast volume, outracing the train at his side, here running in white flights, there whirling in dark pools, while all the black air is filled with its hoarse complaining and explosions of thunderous rage. Now it is a lonely lake, with its beaches and its sedges, its islands and its reflections of sky and cloud and mountain, and its signs of swimming, flying life, which charms him; anon he gazes entranced, amazed, breathless, at a glacier hanging in white, green, flashing loveliness, ten thousand feet above him, or looks with awe upon a valley between two ranges filled for miles and miles with snow to the very peaks, as he remembers that the human race is not so old as that thawless field before him. Such another five hundred miles of traveling is not to be had on the face of the earth. If this strikes the reader as an exaggeration, as it may many — I can only say that it is not. It is a simple statement of an extraordinary fact — a statement which every traveler whose knowledge of the globe is adequate for comparison, who has been over these five hundred miles, will confirm. He who journeys from Kananaskis Falls to Fraser Cañon will experience sensations — however *blasé* with worldwide travel he may be — against which his indurated nerves are not proof.

We four — the Inseparables, as the Man from New Hampshire facetiously called us — left Banff with bright anticipations. Our eyes were as open to see and our spirits as buoyant as if we were boys. We had had a week of pleasure at the " Palace of Delight," as the Judge poetically named the huge hostelry among the mountains, and our last night had been one of rollicking enjoyment. In our dispositions we typed the best habit of Americans when traveling — the habit of self-surrender to the enjoyment of the hour. There can be no question on one point concerning our countrymen. They are the best travelers in the world, not because they travel the most and spend money the freest when journeying, but because they get more knowledge and happiness out of travel than any other people. The inconveniences and deprivations which roughen the temper of the average Englishman only quicken the humor of the Yankee and supply him with entertainment. He travels as a bird flies, utilizing to his enjoyment the opposition of adverse currents, feeds contentedly on the wing, and sleeps restfully on any perch to which the flaws or whirlwinds of unlucky happenings by day or night have gustily blown him. The world likes him and he likes the world, and hence he finds welcome everywhere, and the welcome he gets he thoroughly enjoys. Like a snail, he carries his home around with him on his back, and easily adjusts himself to any condition of shine or shade. The happiest mortal one can meet with is an American in his travels. Speaking but one language and that indifferently well, he hobnobs cheerfully with all nations, uses with the courage of ignorance all languages, and makes fast friends wherever he goes.

We started from Banff in the best of spirits. Had we been in sombre mood, even, the extraordinary vision of beauty and sublimity we beheld would have speedily brightened it, for the sun was just rising above the eastern mountains, and the freshness of morning was on the world and in the air around us. Our course lay along the pebbly banks of the sparkling Bow and up a forest valley. We skirted the Vermilion Lakes and ran along in full view of Mount Massive and the snowy peaks above Simpson's Pass. We whirled around a curve, and the eastern view of Pilot Mountain flashed whitely upon us, and then in a moment the Castle jumped into sight, and we studied with delighted eyes its mighty precipice, its embattled 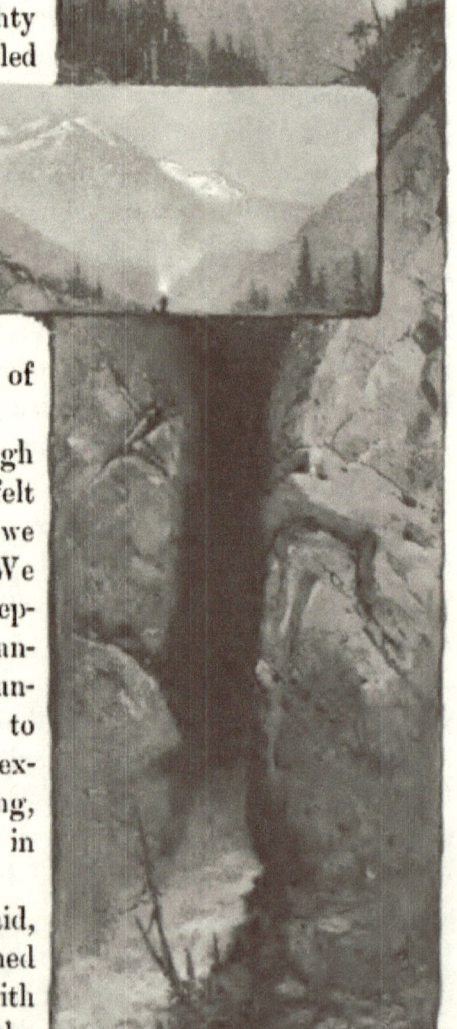 turrets and shapes of fantastic armament.

We were wise enough to be boys. We felt no indifference and we assumed none. We were expectant, receptive, full of happy anticipations, with unjaded nerves, eager to break voice in our excitement as a young, highly bred hound in his first race.

"Judge," I said, looking into his flushed face as he gazed with delighted eyes at the reflection of a mountain in a small lake-like pool lying waveless at its base, "Judge, how old are you this morning?"

"Sixteen, — only sixteen, thank God!" he cried.

"This is my first vacation out of Darmouth," exclaimed Colonel Goffe; and he swung his hat and yelled like a freshman after miraculously passing his first term examination.

We were all looking for the first glacier.

"There it is!" I cried suddenly; and I pointed through the gap towards the lofty peak of Mount Hector.

Like a river it lay, — a river at full flow, which had been frozen solid as it rolled onward and downward; frozen solid and broken off, leaving only a crystallized section exposed to the eye.

It was white, with green lights shot through its fractured and curved extremity, crescent shaped at the end; a monstrous motion suddenly solidified as it plunged downward, and fixed forever in the spot where it hung suspended high up and far off in the air. Above the forest, above the great bulk of the mountain, from the very peak, hung that strange, monumental appearance, a miracle of nature, a mystery of the elements, a wonder to the tourist, like the vision of a poet or a dream of uneasy slumber. Glacier after glacier we saw after that as we rolled onward through this region of marvelous appearances, this land of enchantment, many larger, many higher, many more lovely, more imposing, but none of the hundreds we looked upon later impressed us more powerfully or fixed themselves with deeper impression upon the memory than

CATHEDRAL PEAK.

this first one we saw chained to the crest of Mount Hector.

We were now nearing the summit. The grade rose steeply. The huge engine clomb laboriously upward. It breathed heavily, like a chopper in prolonged effort, when his axe cuts to the centre of the tree and with quickening blood and persistent strokes he delivers each successive blow more fiercely. The cliffs panted back to it. Now and then its circular feet slipped, but it clung desperately to the rails.

"That engine has good grit," said Mr. Pepperell. "How it hangs to it."

"I feel as if I would like to get out and push," replied the Judge.

"Do it, Judge," said the Man from New Hampshire. "I'll sit on this camp stool and hold your coat."

"Colonel Goffe," returned the Judge sternly, "the Court fines you a Reina Victoria for that contemptuous remark."

"All the sentences of this Court end in smoke, I notice," retorted the Colonel, as he handed the Judge his cigar case.

"Here we are at Summit Lake," I exclaimed; and even as I spoke the engine ceased to pant, and the train began to ease itself along swiftly.

How beautiful is a pool among the mountains! Small as it may be, how it can collect and reflect the great world above and around it! It may not be as big as a cliff, and yet a hundred cliffs are in it. A single pine may bridge it, nevertheless it accommodates miles upon miles of forest. Small as it is, the great sun comes and bathes in its depth. Acres of clouds float through it. The sky, the numberless hills with all their countless trees, the mountains so vast, their innumerable peaks, — within its scant space all are grouped and none are crowded. Sweet miracle of the woods, placid mirror of the hills and skies, gentle eye of the forest upon whose clear retina is focused the sublimities of heaven and the beauties of surrounding earth, how often hast thou lost me game and sport because thy loveliness held me pensive at thy grassy rim!

"I wish," cried the Judge, "I wish I could stay a week here and do nothing but sit on the shore of that little lake and gaze into its depths."

"And I wish I could be the artist to sketch you in that position," said Colonel Goffe dryly. "If I should put you in the foreground you would hide the whole lake."

Downward we rolled. We glided smoothly onward as a wing in easy flight cleaves the air.

"This is the poetry of motion," cried the Judge. "We are floating around this mountain's verge as if we were in a balloon."

"Look at this!" Mr. Pepperell exclaimed. "Here is a picture that money can't buy."

We were crossing the gorge of the Wapta River and the sublime scenery which characterizes this section was opening up ahead of us. The train was running very slowly, creeping firmly but carefully along. It seemed to be conscious, and to be clinging tightly and safely to the mountain around whose awful curvature it was making its way with practiced fortitude. It suggested a sailor busily knotting a reef at the yard's end. It is a frightful suspension, but safe — to him. At the right of us the mountain sloped downward sharply a clean thousand feet. To the left it rose nearly sheer upward eight times as far. A black cloud smothered its summit from a hundred gazing eyes. Within its enveloping blackness a glacier lay white, cold, and pulseless in its eternal swoon. Suppose it should be suddenly shocked into life and motion and plunge wildly downward! How it fascinates you to imagine the terrible when you are safe!

To the north a valley, wide, far-reaching, immense, a landscape in itself, unexplored, stretched away in magnificent perspective to distant peaks, white with snow that will never melt. Far up this valley, lifted high among nameless summits standing like grouped spear points, was a glacier, wide as a frozen sea, deep as an ocean, unvisited as yet by man, half of it in black shadow, half flashing with blinding whiteness under the sun, a mute challenge to the courage, the skill, and the science of the continent to come and measure and name it.

Ahead of us Mount Field reared high its black summit. Then rose Cathedral Mount upon us, faded from sight, and came again into view as we glided onward. A majestic, solemn, suggestive presentation of massive bulk and altitude it made, standing out in clear, sharply edged outlines against the blue sky. While above all, loftier, nobler, more varied and impressive, rose the vast mass known as Mount Stephen.

None may describe this mountain. It is not like its fellows round about it. It is not like common mountains. It has an individuality all its own. Our artist has caught its spirit and given a resemblance — but at what a remove from the real Mount Stephen itself. It

is not a mountain to be put in a book, to be printed on a page, to be hung on a wall. Some mountains lend themselves kindly to such patronizing treatment, but Mount Stephen is not of this sort. It cannot be translated from the wilderness and the sky on to canvas. It cannot be snatched from its envelopment of clouds and hung from a peg on a parlor wall. It cannot be coaxed from its native sunshine and shipped to Boston per express. It is a mountain to go to, to visit, to see brilliantly revealed in the sunlight, to gaze at dimly outlined in the dark, to behold in the light of dawn, in the red of sunset, under the stars of night, when the moon clothes it in white splendor from summit to base line. Go and see Mount Stephen so and you shall find in the vision the memory of a lifetime.

CHAPTER XII.

SABBATH AMONG THE MOUNTAINS.

IT was the Sabbath day and we were at Field. With us were a company, tourists like ourselves, who had decided to spend our Sabbath among the mountains, making of it a day of rest in truth. And if among the mountains, where better than at Field, under the shadow of Mount Stephen, and with a multitude of majestic altitudes all around us.

The afternoon was well advanced, and all of us, quite an audience in numbers, were grouped on the piazza, when we saw a gentleman strolling down the track toward the hotel. He was tall, bronzed, and had an Alpine knapsack at his back and a note-book in his hand.

"There! there comes the clergyman we have been

"THERE COMES OUR CLERGYMAN."

praying for all day," cried a young lady to her companion, at my elbow. "There comes our clergyman, and now we can have a regular service; won't that be nice!" And her pink palms met in a way to express the fervor of her religious enthusiasm.

"Jennie, dear," said her companion, a motherly looking lady, "you are always jumping to your conclusions. How do you know the gentleman is a clergyman at all?"

"Ah, I know he is," she reiterated with emphasis.

"But how do you know?" the other insisted.

"Well, because — because — he don't look a bit like one!" she replied.

Nevertheless, in spite of the young lady's assertion, the gentleman who was slowly approaching us did look somewhat like a clergyman. And when he had joined us and we had engaged him in conversation, our impression as to his clerical status was deepened, for he spoke with much feeling and with true spiritual discernment of the religious relations of nature. But whatever doubt remained was suddenly dissipated when he opened his knapsack, for as he did so the leaves of a manuscript closely and careful written were plainly discernible.

"My dear sir," said the Judge, "I cannot but consider your coming as providential. This is the Lord's day, and here we, a company of Christian wanderers, find ourselves spending the holy day among the everlasting hills. We desired to hold a religious service, but are as a flock without a shepherd, for there is not a clergyman among all this large number of tourists.

But now we are, if I mistake not, delivered from our dilemma, for you, my dear sir, are — are you not a clergyman?"

"I am sorry that I am compelled to disappoint you," answered the man, "but I am not a clergyman."

"Not a clergyman!" exclaimed the Judge; "surely, sir, that manuscript there must be" —

"No, that is not a sermon," interrupted the stranger, smiling. "It is only a story."

"I think a story is as good as a sermon, any time," cried the young lady who had been so confident that the new-comer was a clergyman. "And if it isn't too awfully jolly, I wish the gentleman would read it to us. My eyes ache from looking, and I would like to close them and see with my ears, as papa says, for half an hour."

"My dear sir," exclaimed the Judge, "the young lady has voiced my feelings admirably and I doubt not the wishes of the company, and if your story is not of too light a nature, I pray you read it to us, and feel that you are doing us all a positive service. I can promise you, sir, an attentive audience."

"The story I would read you is sober enough for the day," responded the man, "and suggests a theme fit to be meditated on within the shadow of these awful surroundings even; nor will it be of less value because it is of the nature of a personal experience. If you will arrange yourselves to easily hear me, I will gladly read you the story."

In a moment some fifty of us were grouped around the stranger, and certainly no preacher or author ever

ROSS PEAK.

had a more attentive audience than we gave him as he read the strange tale; and surely it would take a long search to find a sermon weighted with a more startling thought. At least, so many of us said at the end of it.

THE TWO GRAVES.

It was in the autumn of 1878, that I found myself riding through that portion of Canada which borders the northern shore of the Ottawa, some hundred miles above its junction with the St. Lawrence. The day was one of a series peculiar to that time of the year and that section of the country. The heat of summer had departed, chilled southward by the advancing frost which the arctic cold had posted in advance to give warning of its approach. But in the valleys and along the hedgerows which skirted the southern exposure of the mountains, the delicious warmth still lingered, as if loth to leave the pleasant haunts where it had so long tarried, happy in the music of the running brooks and the birds that sang in the odorous bushes.

Indeed, it seemed as if here and there it had determined to resist its savage foe; for in nooks where the russet leaves lay thickest and in the wedge-like crevices of ledges it kept almost its August warmth, as if it felt safe to await a fiercer attack behind such formidable barricades.

I had ridden already a goodly distance, and neither I nor my horse was in a mood to hurry; the reins lay loosely on his neck, and he picked his way along the grass-grown path with the leisurely step peculiar to his species when neither their inclination nor that of their riders urge them to a faster gait. Perhaps he as well as I enjoyed not merely the slowness of the pace, but the nature of the surroundings also; for his large, observant eyes studied the flaming bushes as closely as mine, and to his senses the mingled odors of the dying grasses and withered leaves, blended with the fragrance of the evergreens that live on through winter and summer alike, may have been as grateful as they were to mine as I breathed them in.

I had just turned a curve in the road and was descending a gentle slope — a mountain on my left and a stretch of level woodland on my right — when I suddenly came upon a clearing, of some three acres in extent, enclosed by a fence. Age had weakened the settings of the posts, and it no longer kept the trueness of the original lines, but sagged and swayed at different points, while here and there the winds of winter had blown sections of it prone to the ground. The grasses had grown through the palings, and masses of running vines formed over them, whose leaves were now aflame with color.

I instinctively checked my horse to more closely inspect this unexpected opening in the woods, involuntarily looking, as I did so, for the house or the ruins of the house that one day stood, as I naturally supposed, in the clearing; and it was not until I had quite reined my horse into the cleared space, passing through a gap which the winds had made in the enclosure, and looked the field over more closely, that

I discerned that it had never been intended for human habitation, at least not for the habitation of the living, but had rather been set apart for the repose of the dead. The space, in short, into which I had ridden, was a cemetery.

No sooner had I made this discovery than, impelled by curiosity in part, and in part by reverence, I dismounted, and throwing the reins over a post which had once been one of the pillars of the main entrance, I strolled further into the solemn field, with emotions such as would be natural to a man entering a graveyard thus suddenly discovered in the depths of the woods.

"Here," I said to myself, "the former settlers of this once inhabited but now deserted region lie buried. A majestic place for a burial ground, truly;" and I glanced upward at the surrounding mountains which lifted their vast sides round about the vale. "Truly," I continued, "here is a fitting place for the weary to rest after the trials and fatigues of life. The aged who had long borne the heat and burden of the day and they who were suddenly checked in manhood's swift career, husband and wife, parent and child, all could here find the peace which comes after strife, and that sweet rest which waits on human toil. It is pleasant to think that nature, after the fret and fever of life were over, so kindly provided them, amid the very scenes where they toiled and doubtless suffered, a place to repose."

Thus moralizing, I cast my eyes about to discover the number and the grouping of the graves, not doubting I should find many, and with them monumental evidences, of however humble a sort, that affection had remembered them when they had passed away; but to my astonishment I could discover only two graves within the entire enclosure. These were situated side by side, on a slight elevation that swelled its summit near the centre of the enclosure. Confident that further searching would reveal more to me, I made a careful inspection of the field, until I had traversed it from corner to corner and had convinced myself that this strange graveyard was so not only because of its location, a place set apart for the dead where there were none to die, but also because, large as it was, it held but two graves.

"A stranger graveyard than this," I said to myself, "was never seen, for of all the burial places that men ever set apart, of such goodly dimensions as this, I doubt if there be another on the face of the whole earth so sparsely populated: the tenantry of kindred fields is generally crowded enough, and he who has the fortune to occupy a place therein never lacks for neighbors. I will approach the graves and see what memorial affectionate custom has traced upon these lonely slabs." So saying, I drew near to the two graves and proceeded to inspect them more closely.

They were placed some eight feet apart, both facing to the south. It was evident from the size of the mounds that they had been builded for adult bodies, and apparently near the same time. The grasses had matted thickly over both, and a running vine whose main root had sprung from the earth equidistant between the two had sent a branch out impartially toward each. It had grown so luxuriantly that it had embraced either mound, and sent its creeping tendrils even to the top of the two short and narrow slabs of plainly-wrought stone, such as rude skill might easily have quarried from the ledge in the neighboring ravine. It seemed as if nature had, by the growth of her vine, tenderly united in suggestive unity the two mounds, which, standing farther apart and without connection, would have been lonely indeed. "Surely," I said to myself, "this is a quaint and touching spectacle. Only two graves in all this field, and they lying side by side on this little eminence and so affectingly connected. Is there some sweet conscience in nature which forbids her to decorate the one and leave the other unadorned?" And I remembered the saying that the rain falleth alike on the just and unjust. "I doubt not," I continued, "that these two who sleep here were brothers, who had nursed at one maternal breast; who had labored in this vale and on these hills side by side, and who, struck down by death, perhaps simultaneously, were brought by reverential hands in the slow and solemn fashion of the country and with priestly benediction laid side by side. Or perhaps they were two friends strongly attached, some David and Jonathan of this forest glade, who, being so closely united in life as to furnish a proverb of loving companionship, in death were not divided."

Filled with such pleasant imaginings, I kneeled on one of the mounds and with my hand gently moved aside the viney tracery that garnished its white surface with ruddy ornament, in order to read what might be carved beneath.

"James Flynn, aged 60 years, 8 mos. and 9 days. Born April 10th, 17—. Died Nov. 14th, 18—."

I then turned toward the other mound, and kneeling on it lifted the vine from the face of the other slab and read, —

"John Peters, aged 61 years. Born May 19th, 17—. Died Nov. 14th, 18—."

"Buried the same day," I said, rising to my feet. "Buried the same day, and for these thirty years their dust has mouldered side by side. Old men too, honest and honored, I doubt not; brothers they certainly were not, but friends they must have been, or surely they would not have found such close vicinage in death. Old men, who had lived their lives out until the crescent of their youth had come to the full rounded orb of its perfect sphere. Happy in having outlived their passions and the frailties and bitternesses that come therefrom, happy indeed were they," I added, " in having entered, before they came to their tomb, that peace and pleasantness of mood which give to the aged the chiefest beauty of their earthly life and the perfect preparation for the life to come."

While I had thus been pleasantly musing I had almost unconsciously been walking toward my horse, and with my mind still filled with the thought of the two graves I had so suddenly found, and was so soon to leave, I placed my reins on the neck of the animal and my foot in the stirrup, saying as I did so, " I would that I knew the history of the two graves thus so

A MOUNTAIN PICNIC.

strangely placed in this quiet field, and of the two men who have slept and are destined to sleep so long in them side by side."

"I can tell you the history of the two men" —

I turned so suddenly at the unexpected sound of a human voice that the speaker was checked in the midst of the sentence he was uttering. He was a man, old and white headed and bowed with years, for he carried a staff in one hand and was even then leaning heavily upon it. I noticed also that the hand that grasped the stick trembled and shook with that peculiar tremulousness which so often accompanies the weakening of muscular power. Was it something in the fit and color of his garments, was it something in the dignity of his mien, or was it because of the peaceful expression of his countenance? From whichever one of these causes, perhaps from them all combined, I conceived that he belonged to the clergy.

"Reverend sir," said I, releasing my foot from the stirrup and turning toward him, "reverend sir," said I, and I uncovered my head, "I am journeying through the country with a companion who is now on the road some miles behind me, and coming suddenly upon this opening, I observed the two graves yonder and judged that this was a graveyard. Moved by that impulse common to human hearts in so solemn a place, I entered the enclosure to discover what memorials affection had reared above those who sleep. But to my astonishment I have been able to find only two graves in all the field, and I was marvelling, as you interrupted me, at the strange spectacle; so strange that

I doubt if its equal can be found in all the world, the spectacle of a graveyard with only two graves."

"I doubt not," responded the old man, "that your observation is correct, for though I have seen many graveyards myself, and helped to lay many to sleep therein, I know no other allotted to men's final repose in which the number of those who sleep is so small;" and he added, "I would that these were not here, for a sadder lesson than they teach has never been my lot to learn, and the recollection they recall, as I behold them lying here alone, forms one of the saddest memories of my life."

"You speak, reverend sir — for I judge you to be a clergyman — as if you had knowledge of them."

The old man paused a moment before he replied. His eyes were turned toward the two graves, and in them was a far-away look as if they ranged backward across the dim distance of many years; then he added, "I officiated at the service when those two graves were made."

"Indeed," I exclaimed, "indeed! then may I hope to learn something of their history, and how it comes about that only two sleep in this sacred field and they sleep side by side. I should like to know of the lives of those who are its only occupants. Surely there must have been some peculiar history attached to them, — some tender passage in their lives, a life-long sympathy of a notable and noble sort, — to account for the fact that two, who by their names, it would seem, were not akin, should thus be lying in their last sleep like brothers, inseparable even in death."

"Your surmises are far from correct," replied the venerable man. "They were not brothers, as you have suggested, they were not even friends, they were bitter enemies."

"Enemies!" exclaimed I, "enemies! great heavens! How came they then to be buried side by side?"

"Your astonishment is but natural," was the answer. "It was strange, it was unnatural, it was even irreverent, but it was in accordance with their wish, — I may say their express command."

"I pray you," said I, rehitching my horse at the post, "I pray you, if your leisure permits, tell me the tale, for certain it is that my mind cannot conceive why two enemies should desire to be buried side by side. Surely human life is long enough to exhaust the force of human hatred; or is it a part of that fierce fire which is never quenched, not even by the waters of death, or the smothering dampness of the grave?"

"I will comply with your request," responded the aged man, "for I am weary with walking and would willingly rest a little space before I pursue my way. You must know, then," he continued, as he seated himself on a stone opposite me, "you must know that I visited this place partly that I might see once more the beauties of nature in this secluded spot, and partly that my eyes might behold again the scenes that were once so familiar and, I may add, so grateful to them.

"Thirty years ago this little vale, now so reposeful, resounded with the hum of human activity. In yonder mountain side you can find a shaft sunk by the miners' skill, in search of the rich ores which were then believed to lie buried within its sides. Here, in the depths of the forest, a village sprang up, as it were in a day, and men of many nationalities came pouring into this secluded glen in what proved to be a vain search for gold. Providence guided me to this spot, even with the first wagon train that penetrated here, and here I stayed and ministered the best I might to their eternal good, until the last wagon left the glen forever. Ah, those were stirring and noisy times," mused the old man, as if he once more saw the bustle and heard the noise of the busy encampment. "A hundred axes swept the mighty trees from yonder slope, and half a hundred cabins rose as by magic on the banks of yonder brawling stream. The giant pines that then stood where is now this clearing furnished the walls of their habitations, and from yonder rock, by which that aged beech-tree stands, I preached the best I might, to those who came seeking earthly wealth, of that other treasure which neither moth nor rust can corrupt, nor thieves break through and steal."

"I do not doubt," I said, as the venerable man paused a moment in the recital of his early efforts to lead men to be wise, "that your endeavors were as successful as I feel they were earnest."

"They were not wholly in vain," replied the other reverently, "for I had the everlasting word and the spirit that quickeneth to assist me, and even the foolishness of preaching did not wholly fail. For with two exceptions the toilers in the mines and they who tilled the open spaces, where nature made tillage possible, lived in peace one with another and outwardly, at least, kept the laws of God.

"I said all but two; these two were men of another country and another clime. Both were dark of face and mood, and scarred in unknown fights. It was whispered that they had met in deadly conflict years before, and that the scars of each were of wounds made by the other. But none knew, perhaps, for certain, for they were of a sort little given to speech and told their history to none.

"That they hated each other they did not conceal, and their hatred was of that quiet and deadly sort most painful to see. They were not loved by any. They were even shunned by those with whom they toiled. Indeed, they were the dark spirits of the camp, for it might scarce be called a settlement, and their presence was universally regretted; and yet they made no disturbance; but whether from the peculiar orderliness of their surroundings or because each with the patience of deadly cunning bided his time, there was no outbreak between them.

"For two years they worked side by side. By a strange fortune, for the cabins were built in common and then drawn for by lot, the one drew No. 20, and the other 21, and so they lived side by side in silent hatred."

"It was a terrible way to live," I remarked, for the strange tale interested me deeply, "and certainly a stranger fortune never befell two foes, than to thus meet in a foreign land, scarred by each other's blows, and toil side by side by day and live in houses that almost touched, hating each other with terrible hatred, and yet never exchanging word or blow."

" It was, indeed," returned the old man, " a terrible way indeed, and I did what I could to bring them to a better mind. God knows I labored with them and strove in prayer in their behalf; but my labor was in vain, and my prayers, for some wise purpose, were never answered, for their hearts remained hardened, and I could make no salutary impression on their wicked souls.

" The mines, which at first had been productive, suddenly gave out and no longer paid the expenses of working them. And at the end of two years they were abandoned and the settlement prepared to disperse. When scarcely a dozen remained and these, myself among the number, were preparing to follow those who were already gone, the two men, who had made no preparations to go and were evidently intending to remain, for the purpose, I doubt not, of meeting once more in savage conflict with none near to thwart their deadly intent, were suddenly taken sick. Humanity forbade that we should desert them, and we tarried until the end should appear, but their sickness was unto death, and we had not long to wait.

" They died the same night. The one but a few moments before the other. I attended at their death beds, but had no other reward than the consciousness of duty done. The one that died first showed no concern save for one thing; asked but one question, Would the other die? A brother miner standing by his side answered, ' He will not live an hour.'

" For an instant the light of a wild, fierce satisfaction blazed balefully from the eyes that were already half

EAST OTTERTAIL.

eclipsed behind the shadow of death, and in what seemed to us to be an imprecation breathed in an unknown tongue, the wretched man straightened himself in his bed, and with the deadly scowl still on his face, and the passing curse still quivering on his lips, died. It was a terrible scene, sir."

"It must have been," I exclaimed, "it must have been; but did the other show no repentance?"

"None whatever," was the mournful reply. "From the presence of the dead I went to the presence of the dying. A miner who had worked by his side in the shaft, and was in some sort a comrade, was standing by his cot as I drew near. Life was fast ebbing away, and what might be done must be done quickly. I begged that I might pray with him. He refused. I gently urged him to repentance. He smiled in mockery. Suddenly starting from the deadly stupor settling on him, he asked the miner if his enemy were living. He was told that the man had even then died. A look of fiendish satisfaction flashed through the gloom of his swarth face, and lifting his clenched fists he brought them down, smiting the couch with dying energy, as if it were the head of his foe.

"'Have you any wish to leave behind you?' asked his comrade.

"'Yes,' he answered, and the words were hissed from between his teeth with indescribable fierceness. 'Yes. Make my grave close beside his, damn him.'

"It was a terrible scene, a terrible scene," exclaimed the old man, and for a moment he hid his face in his hands as if the distance of thirty years were not enough to shut it from his eyes. At length he resumed,—

"Unnatural and terrible as it was, we felt constrained, at least the miners did, to obey the dying behest; and so on the morrow the men who had hated each other in life, and hated each other in death, were buried side by side."

The old man paused at this point a moment, evidently oppressed by the memory of human passion and wickedness he had been narrating. At length his eyes wandered toward the two graves which nature had so impartially adorned, and upon which nature's sun was now shining so kindly, and he added, —

"There have they slept these thirty years, side by side, unknown and unnoted, save by some chance traveler like yourself. And there will they sleep until the resurrection trump shall sound and they shall rise at its commanding summons."

"Surely," I exclaimed, "surely that morn will not find them in their hatred. Surely, reverend sir, you cannot believe that when the trumpet of the Lord shall sound, and men come forth in obedience to its call, these two shall rise with the old hatred in their souls?"

"I cannot tell as one who speaks from knowledge," answered the old man, "but I have studied the characters of men these sixty years, and noted the laws that seemed to underlie their changes, but have seen nothing to warrant the belief that character, once settled and confirmed, ever changes. Habits change, men acquire new expression for their powers, but the character itself remains permanent and solidly fixed as the everlasting hills, unless previous to death a change is wrought by the Spirit through repentance."

"But, sir," I exclaimed, "does death, then, do nothing for us, and does the grave not bring a cooling to the fierce heat of human passion? Surely one might judge by the way in which men of your profession speak at funeral scenes, that at the close of life, even in the act of its closing, there comes to men a needed and a blessed correction. Certainly I have heard them so express themselves, and I myself have found comfort in the faith that amid the darkest clouds of death the mourner's eye could always see a star."

"I know that under the pressure of the scene, and of that humane desire, strong in every sympathetic heart, to speak some word that can console the present grief," answered the old man, "that my brethren do thus speak at funerals. And I myself have often been prompted to do the same and have often done it, but I am confident that the impulse of the moment was not born of reason and had no warrant in the Scripture, for the Scripture saith, 'As the tree falls so shall it lie,' and again, 'Let him who is filthy be filthy still.' And in these sayings, God does not, as I conceive, speak judgments on men, but simply asserts the permanence of human character, which, amid whatever of ruin may have come to it, retains at least the dignity of being true unto itself."

"What hope is there for man, then?" I cried out; "for if no blessed change may come and all must be in the hereafter even as they are here, if not swift mercy matches the swiftness of the fatal stroke, how can the eternal Father adjust the feelings of his bosom to mortal circumstance? Venerable man, it is not for me, who am untaught in doctrine, to argue with one like you, clerically trained and wise with years, but eternity is long and life is short. The cradle and the grave are ever in sight, and short the space and swift the passage from the one to the other. Must there not be at the end something to match the love that watched over us in the beginning, some sweet forgiveness to hover on tireless wing above our growing faults, some wisdom to constantly point out and some love to persuade us unto good, and in the end, if necessary, some almighty mercy to wipe, with one brave gesture of atoning pity, the stains of all our faults and sins away? Say, reverend man, does no such divine provision exist?"

It is but just to say that the old man was profoundly affected by the appeal, which, in the depth of my longing for human kind thus stirred, I had poured forth with unconscious earnestness. He actually groaned aloud, as if on his spirit, which it needed but a glance at his benevolent face to see was full of sweetest pity for all the erring, there rested the Atlas-like load of human destiny. He groaned aloud, and rising from the rock on which he had been resting, he lifted his aged face to the skies and with tears marking their course down his wrinkled cheeks, he said: —

"The heavens are full of mercy, that I know, and motherhood without sex divides, at least, with sterner elements the throne. But man is a mighty being; he is too great to change or be changed, save by his own volition, and when once the character is formed, when the tree has firmly rooted itself and clasped the moveless rock beneath, — how shall it change? Whence shall come the wish to change? How out of concentrated evil shall be born the holy purpose? But young man," he added, as he took my hand, " you are young, and I would not dim a single hope that lights the world ahead of you, nor would I dispel any happy illusion, even, that may solace your grief when grief shall come. For even illusions, if they be comforting, may serve a divine purpose. No, no, live happily, in hopeful thoughts of men, for hope is often truer than logic. But these men were matured. Their minds fully made up, they died impenitent; aye, resisting overtures of mercy, they went into the grave mutually resisting each other. What is there in that silence yonder?" and he pointed his long finger toward the little eminence on which the two graves were, " what is there in the silence of their long sleep there to change them? Do men change their natures in slumber? Do they not rise as they lie down? The trump will sound. Those graves will open. Those sleepers there will wake — wake from their long sleep, and I fear they will wake hating each other still. For hatred lives with the immortality of all ill;" and with these words the old clergyman bade me good-by and turned away.

For a moment his eyes studied the surrounding mountains as if they were taking their long and affectionate farewell; for a moment he stood and listened to the soft, musical lapsing of the stream that murmured through the glade, and then, supported by the staff he held, with feet that brushed the ruddy and rustling leaves aside as they walked on, he passed slowly up the lane and disappeared from view.

My conversation with the old clergyman had given me ample food for meditation. The strange history he had told and the fearful supposition he had advanced possessed my mind to the exclusion of any other subject. The loneliness of the secluded spot, when he had retired, seemed lonelier than before he had joined me. The two graves seemed to deepen the solitude. They no longer suggested human companionship, but alienation, and between the two I seemed to see a great gulf fixed, deep and wide, such as relentless and interminable enmity digs between two souls. Would Heaven's mercy ever bridge a gulf like that, or would it yawn unbridged forever? Was the old man right? Is human hatred immortal? Is there no solvent in the grave to check its eating corrosion or wash its deepening stain away? Thus I, pondering, questioned destiny, and pushed my thoughts out into the eternities. How many have questioned thus. But has any human eye ever seen the stony lips of this dreadful sphinx open in answer, or has any human ear ever heard a sure response?

The sun shone warmly along the mountain side and showered the lonely opening with its beams. The leaves were yellow and thick at my feet, and my faithful horse dozed at his post. "I will wait for the coming of my companion," I said, and casting myself amid the warm leaves I leaned back against a moss-covered stone, and thus, half reclining, fell asleep.

What are dreams? Are they prophecies? Were the

THE CHANCELLOR.

old prophets only dreamers? Are they senseless movements of the thinking faculty? What becomes of the mind when we sleep? Does it sleep too, or is it able to receive impressions, which the slumbering senses are then unable to report? Are the visions that come to it mere fantasies, void of truth or reason? Who can tell? I only know that I slept, and sleeping dreamed. And in that dream I was changed myself, and saw such changes in earth and men that I seek in vain for words with which to describe them.

I said I was changed. I was. I was grown out of and above my old self and had become a new being. New sight was mine, new hearing; I could see everywhere: I could hear everything. I ruled space. No sound, no motion escaped me. It was marvellous. This is the best I can do to describe the change in me.

I said I saw changes. I did. There was no horizon to my vision. My sight was circular, and my eyes flashed great zones of observation round the globe instantly. How active men were, and how idle! How sad, and how merry! I saw them being born, I saw them dying. Some were praying, some were carousing, some were dancing, some were fighting; and the mighty murmur of all their noises, their sobbing and their laughing, their groaning and their cheering, their praying and their cursing, as it swelled up from the earth and rolled its waves of sound around the globe, came collectively and individually into my ears, even as ordinary sound is heard by us in waking moments. What a capacity I was, while like a god I lay, seeing the whole world and hearing all its varied noises. Does the body dwarf us so? Does it bind us with withes of limitation as the Philistines did Samson; and is death but the snapping of the cords in the severance of which there comes back to us the mighty and original strength? I wonder.

Suddenly, even as I was looking with this all-perceiving vision, and listening with this all-receiving sense of hearing, silence fell on the world. Not a noise; not a voice; not a whisper. The guns of war were dumb. Men were dumb. Volcanoes were smothered by their last explosion and their craters yawned silently. The waves stiffened and stood rigid. Birds, checked in mid flight, hung fixed, as if nailed to the sky. All living things stood still. The hush of an awful expectation fell on the world.

Next, darkness! Darkness dense, instant, impenetrable. No sun, no moon, no star, no taper, no spark. The darkness did not come, — it was. The sun did not fade, — the moon did not wane. The stars did not grow dim by degrees. The fires of the earth did not pale. The candles did not flicker — all lights, on the instant, in the twinkling of an eye, exploded and went out. No noise, no light. Silence and darkness over all the earth!

The world listened. Nature hid her face and waited. What was coming?

A noise, a sound as of many waters! A peal as of a mammoth bell rung by mighty and invisible hands in an invisible belfry! A blast: a trumpet note, blown by immeasurable power; a note round, full, immense, that captured the universe and filled it so that its very borders rang! *The last trump!*

The field in which I lay shook. A thrill as of awful terror ran through the sod. The turf seemed to creep and shrivel with fear. The two graves opened. The two men rose, and each standing in his coffin looked at the other, the same — great God! — the very same as when they died! They had slept a thousand years, ten thousand, but all the years had not changed them a whit, for the same hatred glared in their faces as they stood in the resurrection as when they died, cursing each other in the cabins that stood by the gurgling stream. Yea, there they were, unchanged by all the years that had come and gone since their bodies had been buried side by side, in that little clearing in the Canadian woods, ten thousand years before!

"Do those wretches know what an eternity there is before them?" I said to myself, as I gazed in horror at the spectacle. "I will go and plead with them," and I was on the point of starting up when I felt a shock — a terrible shock — as if the solid earth had exploded, and then another more terrible than the former. I screamed, my eyes sprang open.

"Wake up! wake up!" It was my companion who was shaking me.

"Wake up; what are you dreaming about, old boy?"

Thank God, it was a dream! Thank God, nothing but a dream. Perhaps the old pastor was wrong, perhaps men do change, — perhaps.

CHAPTER XIII.

THE GREAT GLACIER.

"I will lift up mine eyes unto the hills."

SWEEPING around the point of a nameless mountain, we glided into the dim, narrow vista of a snow-shed, five hundred yards, perhaps, in length. Here and there its gloom was crossed with shafts of light and checkered with gleaming rays, which made of the long vista a kaleidoscope of jet-black blocks bordered by bright, many-colored lines, changeful and lively, presenting to the gazer's eye a lovely picture to look upon; while far beyond, the aperture stared at us like a great white, expressionless eye, at which we rushed with rattle and roar and burst of thunderous sound from wheel and truck, hissing brakes and belching funnel, but which, unfrightened, stared steadily at us without shrinking as we came hurtling on. In a moment we were shot out of the monstrous tunnel, framed with gigantic timbers, strongly braced as is the curvature of the world, on which the avalanche falls harmless, and over whose roof, angled truly to the mountain slope and riveted into its side, the awful landslide, wide and long with the width and length of acres, its trees all standing and its huge bowlders undisturbed, pours its vast mass into the ravine below, leaving this magnificent device of man's invention unshaken and unstirred.

Onward we whirled, the majestic forest trees on either side. Upon our left a mountain slope, wide, high lifted, an immense stretch of sylvan surface; on our right a dark, deep ravine, down whose black bottom a glacial torrent drew its foaming line; when suddenly our engine curved sharply to the right, and lo, a spectacle of spectacles stood full before our wondering eyes.

"Heavens!" exclaimed the Judge excitedly, "was there ever such a sight?"

Those who have traveled, who have wandered far and seen much, will tell you that out of the mass of things, places and faces they have seen, a few alone remain fixed and clearly outlined in memory. Many are the pictures we hang on memory's walls, but with the passage of time most fade to blackness. Only a few hold their colors fast, and fewer yet brighten them as the years go on : here an ocean scene, a storm, a drifting wreck lightning-lighted, or scudding like the ghost of a ship through the tempestuous moonlight; or it may be a face, — a single face, old or young, happy or sad, living or dead, a friend's, a foe's, a stranger's; a stretch of forest, a mountain view, a torrent bursting from some savage gorge down which Chaos hurriedly trailed, followed by her unformed remnants when driven from the face of the earth by the growing order of the skies. So travelers testify, and

thus we who gazed, gray-headed wanderers all of us, knew it would be with this spectacle which stood in start-

THE GREAT GLACIER.

ling clearness before our eyes, and which had risen into view on the instant from the depths of the savage Selkirks. It was a picture as clearly cut as some old cameo edged by that antique skill that now is dead; as pronounced in the lines of its drafting as strongly contrasting colors in nature might make it: so varied in the figures introduced, so strange and even startling in the grouping of its related parts, that upon the instant it dominated the mind and boldly challenged forgetfulness.

"Never did I see such a picture," said Mr. Pepperell in a low voice, "never, not even on the Fraser or the Thompson in the old days!"

And this is the picture we saw, translated from its majesty and glories down to the paltry measurement and dull neutrality of petty, colorless words: —

A little plat rescued from chaos by man's love of order; a level space of scant size, made by ironing out the corrugation of the hills; on this little platform, or plateau of level space, a cottage, unique in style, neither house nor chalet, but fitting harmoniously to the landscape; in front, a space graveled and platted for flowers, — a summer garden in miniature. In the centre of it a fanciful fountain jetted its glacial spray upward, where the wind caught it, and blew it at random through the bright sunlight, so that in flying and falling it filled all the air with broken pearls, fragments of silver, and sparklings of prismatic fire. Far below this scant level space, with its graveled walks, flashing fountain, and widely verandahed miniature mansion, dropped a gorge through which a glacial torrent whirled its white line of hoarse noise. Sheer upward lifted the opposite mountain, a full ten thousand feet, its bold summit of steel gray rock well named Eagle Peak, for only an eagle's wing might reach it.

Down its imposing front a torrent foamed from top to base. Slowly through the long, lofty distance our admiring eyes swept their gaze until they rested upon the buttressed battlements of Sir Donald, which, pointed like a pyramid, interrogates the mysteries of star and sky, the golden course of wheeling orbs, and the meaning of that blue depth and distance which lie level, serene, and still, above the storms which vex the lower atmospheres.

"That monstrous shaft," said the Judge, as we all stood gazing at Sir Donald, "is a solemn interrogation of what is above and beyond."

"Look at this," said Mr. Pepperell calmly, as he faced about.

In the rear of the chalet a magnificent forest growth swelled loftily upward, symmetrical, proportionate, a lovely, harmonious whole, — a sylvan picture, vast of height, framed by the sky in massive blue, and fretted along its edges with scuds of mist and changeful drifts of cloud. Never had the eye of one of us wood wanderers seen a lovelier exhibition of forest growth; abundant, dense, soft-toned, untouched by fire, unscarred by violence of slide or avalanche; a landscape scene of unmatched perfection.

Slowly our eyes wandered down the pass and clomb the Hermit Range, peak by peak, stole along its slopes of ice, and crept beneath the glaciers, filling every

MT. HERMIT, ROGERS PASS.

THE GREAT GLACIER. 267

gorge, hanging poised ready to drop, or held, jammed in the vast amphitheatres where they have been held beyond the count of years, and where they will remain, unmoved, unmelted, until time is ended or the present order of creation passes away.

So we stood steadfastly gazing at the vast vision, enraptured, when an exclamation from a man behind us faced us around, and there, to the north and east, we saw a sight which may not, perhaps, be matched in its grandeur and surroundings on this earth of ours. A glacier, vast, lofty, immense, buttressed, fissured, creviced, — a section of the Mississippi tilted up obliquely and frozen solid; the St. Lawrence pouring bodily over a mountain range ten thousand feet above you and turned on the instant into ice, stiffened solid at its maddest plunge; a creation of ten thousand years; a monument above those past, dead years, which all the rain and shine of other equal years to come will not efface; standing cold, monstrous, motionless, silent, sublime, within a distance so short from our parlor car that even the weakest woman or smallest child in it might, by an easy stroll, stand under its ponderous front. Heavens! how small, how feeble, how insignificant seemed the engine of our heavy train, with its sobs, and pantings, and puny puffs of power, beside that monstrous creation of ages, that landscape of frozen force, that overhanging world of chained energy which, should Nature ever loosen the chilled links which chained it to that mountain pass, would sweep our engine, train, and yonder house away like chips; ay, crush, grind and pulverize them all to finest dust, so fine that, were it dry, the winds might lift it as they lift ashes and blow it through the air, invisible to mortal eye.

"Never shall it be said," exclaimed the Judge, "that I came to such an environment of majesty as this and passed heedlessly on. Here we will stop a day and a night, and see the sunset splendor and the sunrise glory on these peaks, and the moonlight whiten the surface of that frozen field. There is not ice enough in Switzerland to make that single glacier yonder. Let the train move on. We four have wandered on the earth too widely and seen too many of its wonders not to recognize the extraordinary and do homage to it."

And so the train rolled down the grade, around the swell of the mountain beyond, and left us four gray-headed boys standing above the glacial torrent, gazing and wondering.

That afternoon we took the trail — an easy way, which led us to the Glacier's front. Slowly we drew our line of progress toward it. The fit mood was on us all. We were alone, we four. We were intelligent enough to appreciate the awful phenomenon. We saw it with the eyes of many years. We could measure it by European comparison. We could weigh it in the scales of world-wide knowledge. Two of us had footed the Alpine passes. One had seen the Himalayas. Another had wintered within the Arctic Circle.

Slowly we moved forward. A few rods of motion onward, and we would pause. We were all eyes, all feeling. We felt we were approaching a fragment of eternity. We were drawing nigh to, and gazing at, a bit of the everlasting. Before us was the work of ages. Here the centuries had stopped. Between these monstrous mountains, Time had come to a full halt, powerless to go one foot farther. Here before us, with folded wings, white-faced, hoary-headed, his scythe held in his stiffened hands, we saw him stand, a statue of ice.

"Older than Rome, older than Egypt, older than Man!" murmured the Judge solemnly, as he gazed.

In front of the Glacier was a great round wall of sand, of cobbles, of bowlders. Its pressure drove downward to the bed rock of the world, and ploughed the surface earth.

"This plough ploughs slowly, but it ploughs deep," remarked Colonel Goffe, as he ran his eye along the huge ridge.

"Think who steadies it!" said the Judge.

The sun sank from sight behind the western ridge. The gray shaft of Sir Donald flushed, reddened, then blazed as with fire.

From amid the dark firs above us Night softly shook her raven plumage, and feathered us with gloom. Then she spread her sable wings. She soared upward, and the world darkened. Anon she sailed, a vast formation of blackness above the peaks. The skies saw her coming and welcomed her with every window lighted. The Indian myth was realized. The Raven brooded the world.

But the great Glacier amid the gloom still showed whitely. From between the pillars of darkness, from the cavernous blackness of night, it looked forth like the face of a dead man from the mouth of a grave.

"Older than Night, and hence stronger!" whispered the Judge.

Thus we four sat in the darkness watching and pondering, while through the gloom and the stillness the glacial torrent at our feet tore its line of hoarse noise.

"See!" I exclaimed. "The Glacier is growing whiter. Its paleness begins to brighten. Look! There is a gleam in that upper crevice! And see — see that flash of white!"

"The moon! The moon!" cried the Judge. "The moon is rising. Now we shall see the spectacle of a lifetime!"

Excuse me, reader, I cannot write it down. I know the limitation of letters. Even could I tint them with all the colors of the palette, it were in vain. Imagine our position, standing in that gorge, deep, deep down at the very roots of those monstrous mountains, within the inclosure of their awful environment; the stillness, which the roar of the torrent divided, but did not disturb; the whole world black with the blackness of night when it smothers the woods out of sight of the eye; the great Glacier in front of us, vast, monstrous, formless, as it lay dimly outlined in the gloom; then imagine it growing, growing, growing upon the sight. See it brighten and widen out into view.

See the gleams begin to run over it. See that flash of white fire strike the crest and run crinkling along the lofty ridge until it connects the two opposite peaks with a line of living light.

See the crevices gleam and glisten brighter and brighter. Behold the sparkles and flashes of fire start

MOUNT SIR DONALD.

up here and there, at random, flash, shift and fade, and then, as the rounded orb, vast of size, intense, rose majestically above the summit and looked calmly, and, as

it seemed, admiringly down upon it, behold, in your imagination, what we saw, — the monstrous mountains darkly forested round about us, between which, wide as a landscape, lay the great Glacier, bathed in soft white radiance from side to side, from base to summit, and above it the dome of the sky, and suspended from it the round moon!

"Day unto day uttereth speech, and night unto night showeth knowledge," said the Judge reverently, and we turned slowly from the sublime spectacle before us, and started to pick our way carefully down the trail.

We had seen the Glacier! It was enough.

CHAPTER XIV.

THE HERMIT OF FRASER CAÑON.

> "We are not ourselves,
> When nature, being oppressed, commands the mind
> To suffer with the body."

HE who attempts to describe in words this majestic exhibition of nature, advertises his ignorance of the limitation of letters and his lack of artistic discernment. Even the tongue of Pericles, with its perfect command of the Grecian vocabulary, would have faltered and grown dumb had he stood where we stand, and attempted to describe what we see."

It was the Judge who spoke, as we stood grouped at a point midway between the extremities of the Great Cañon.

"Nevertheless, there are those who expect me to do it," I remarked, "and will hold me at fault if I fail."

"Never you mind that," responded the Judge, speaking with emphatic earnestness. "Be true to your knowledge of language and your own sense of the fit and the modest. Here is a work of God whose wildness and awful sublimity is not only beyond verbal description, but so far beyond it that only scribblers would attempt it. Here is one of the rare exhibitions of the world. Niagara matches it in nature. The Halls of Karnac and the Great Pyramid are to be classed with it among the works of men. I have walked through the one, and camped a week at the base of the other. This exhibition makes me hold my breath. If the world would learn what is here, let them come and see it. How can you describe that mad turmoil of water? How picture, with your pen, this awful environment of mountains? Can you portray this terrible gloom, or put upon your pages that far-off gleam of ice on those summits, or send through the leaves of your book the hoarse roar of yonder whirling, thundering flood? Let your artist attempt it if he must. His failure will demonstrate the powerlessness of the pen. Victor Hugo himself would close his note-book were he here. Lay down your portfolio, and we will sit on this rock, and see the day shrink out of this fearful gorge, and the night push her black columns into it."

We four were together. We had left the car at

Yale, and followed the old government road up the cañon. The day was warm, and we had decided to camp one night beside the terrible river which flows wide and deep, swift and strong, with rush and hiss and roar as of thunder, between the cliffs which lift their ridges to the stars.

"Had the old Greeks known this," said the Judge, sententiously, as we sat on the ledge, gazing at the mad

EAGLE PEAK.

river, — "they would have made it the entrance to Hades. Here is such a Styx and Acheron as they never dreamed of."

"Charon could never have ferried a stream like that," I said, pointing to the whirling water below.

"They would have made him go with the current," responded the Judge. "Down with the current that old freighter of souls would have gone, — down between those ledges and through those ghastly heaps of foam, out of sight, with his pale passengers, forever and ever."

Nothing beyond this for a long time was said. We sat in silence, — we four, — all eyes, all ears, all feeling. We heard the roar of the river rise mightily and hoarsely up between the cliffs. It was that of a lion sounding in the solitude of the desert or amid the ruins of a tenantless city half buried in desert sand. We saw the light shrink and fade from the gorge as that of life shrinks and fades from the glassing eyes of the dying. We saw the day, pallid with fear, climb the cliffs, as if stricken with terror at the growing gloom below, frantic to reach their tops and rush with headlong haste after the declining sun. We watched the gloom spread over the river, and the white of its rage flash fitfully through it as it deepened. We saw the darkness gather and grow dense along the great forested slopes above, and sway out, like black fog, from either side of the chasm, until it met the middle air. And then through the smother of gloom we saw the heavens make revelation of glorious globes, of flashing orbs and shining worlds, — proof that above and beyond this awful gorge, this chasm of Chaos, this cave of Night, the universe of law and light still held its brilliant course and kept its benignant movements wheeling steadily on.

"I trust," said Mr. Pepperell, as he arose from the rock, "that I am not unmindful of these august surroundings, and I shrink from rudely disturbing your reflections, but I confess that I am as hungry as a bear, and if Colonel Goffe will help me find some cones I will start a fire, and we will see what we have in the hamper for supper."

What a repast we four old campers had that night! Our fire was kindled on a wide, flat ledge, which projected slightly over the river. Above us, two giant firs rose loftily. Below us, the river seethed and flashed. Across the whirling current our campfire built its shifting, tremulous shaft of red blood color.

We broiled a ten-pound salmon which an Indian had speared for us, as we strolled up the road that afternoon. Our provisions were ample, and we feasted our hunger full. And when the meal was made we sat and fed the fire with fresh cones and sticks, and talked, — talked gravely, as men of sense so circumstanced might.

"I met with a strange experience here a year ago," said Mr. Pepperell, suddenly, "and one of my motives for taking this journey was to visit this cañon and this very spot where we are. As strange an experience as ever befell a man," he added musingly.

"Tell us of it," cried the Judge, earnestly; "tell us your tale of the cañon. We did not visit this awful gorge to sleep, but to see, listen, and feel; and a strange tale told at midnight, amid these surroundings, would be most apropos indeed."

"It is not so much a story as an experience," replied Mr. Pepperell, "strange and wild enough to suit this spot and hour, and which you can all share with me if you choose. It will be an encore to me, but a novelty to you."

"What do you mean?" interrogated the Judge, in a surprised tone. "I don't understand you, sir."

In place of direct reply, Mr. Pepperell said:—

"Do you know, Colonel Goffe, that you are sitting on as strange a tablet as the hand of man ever traced before he died, to trouble the world after he died?"

"Jupiter Crickets!" cried the Colonel, as he jumped to his feet, "what do you mean, Mr. Pepperell?"

"I will show you what I mean," he replied. "And I will show you what I found here a year ago. Yes, we will go through the same experience together that I went through alone, and you shall tell me what you think of it; whether he was mad, and how he died, and where he lies buried?"

"Of whom are you talking," cried the Judge, excitedly, for the suddenness with which Colonel Goffe had risen and Mr. Pepperell's mysterious words had excited all of us. "Man alive! of whom are you talking?"

"Of the *Hermit of Fraser Cañon*," responded Mr. Pepperell; "that is what I call him, because that is what he calls himself. Look here," and he began to brush the leaves and moss from the stone upon which

Colonel Goffe had been sitting, "what do you make of that? You are a trailer," and he looked up at me. "Can you translate that sign?" And behold, as we looked, we saw chiseled into the ledge the following symbols and figures.

"Easily enough," I responded, as my eye caught the tracing clearly in the light of a torch I held over it. "It means, go one hundred and fifty feet in a straight line from this spot towards yonder cliff. Then two hundred feet at nearly right angles to the left; then eighty feet obliquely, and you will come to a cabin. The curved lines are only intended to deceive and bewilder. He converted his straight lines into a labyrinth to deceive."

"Well done," exclaimed Mr. Pepperell, "you have read at sight what it took me a week to decipher. By chance I built my fire here, and in the light of it I saw that rude tracing in the ledge. It puzzled me. It tormented me. It threw me into a fever of curiosity. I studied it for days and nights, and at last I got the cue. Gentlemen, we will now do what I did one night, last year. I want you to see this ' *cabin* ' and what is in it. Will you come?"

"Certainly," I answered. "But, Mr. Pepperell," I continued, a year brings avalanches in this country, and I warrant your ' *cabin* ' won't look as when you saw it."

"The cabin which that ' C ' stands for was built by a Builder whose buildings never fall. Judge, take those two candles. Colonel Goffe, you carry the lantern. Mr. Murray, you and I will take a torch. Here, let me go ahead. I have measured this line before." And with this he started carefully on, we following.

Slowly, with the aid of our lighted torches, we worked our way toward the cliff for the one hundred and fifty allotted feet. Then Mr. Pepperell ran the line two hundred feet to the left. His memory had evidently retained a vivid remembrance of the trail, for he hesitated at no point of it. At the end of the two hundred feet he turned obliquely to the left, and the eighty feet brought us to the very front of the gigantic cliff.

"Where is your *cabin?* " I cried exultantly, not doubting but that a snow slide had swept it into the Fraser. "Where is the cabin that the ' C ' stands for on the diagram, Mr. Pepperell?"

"Here it is," he responded promptly. "Look!"

and he lifted his torch to the face of the cliff and, lo! there, painted on the front of the rock was a letter "C"!

An exclamation escaped us as we crowded close up to the ledge to inspect it.

It was a monstrous letter, at least three feet in its perpendicular length and fully two feet across. It was painted in some gray mixture which nearly matched the color of the rock, and was not discernable save upon close inspection. It was enlarged at the back of it, and united at the curved extremities so that it rudely resembled the shell of a clam even as our artist has drawn it.

"What in the world does this mean, sir?" I exclaimed, looking at Mr. Pepperell.

His response to this interrogation was singularly direct and instructive. He took a chisel-shaped instrument from one pocket, and a hammer from another, and placing the edge of the sharp steel at the central point of the letter, where the lines connected the extremities, struck it sharply with the hammer, and a section of the rock coincident with the painted form of the letter stirred, and we saw that it was only a cunningly devised door fitted to an aperture in the ledge.

"Great heavens!" I cried, "the C of the diagram by the river does not mean *cabin* at all, but a *cave!*"

"Precisely," returned Mr. Pepperell complacently. "It took me a long time, but I guessed the trick at last. Gentlemen, will you enter the hermit's cave?" And he stepped through the strange door while we followed.

THE HERMIT OF FRASER CAÑON.   285

The sensation we experienced as we passed through that strangely-contrived entrance and stood in the mysterious apartment can better be imagined than described. We were too astonished at what we saw to

say a word. We stood and gazed in silent amazement at what we beheld revealed by the light of lantern, candle, and torch.

The cave was of large size, larger than an ordinary chamber. In the centre stood a table strongly constructed, the legs of which were grotesquely carved. Skill, patience, and artistic cleverness had wrought out its strange and ludicrous designs. On the smooth surface of it a clown's head was curiously traced, the face of which was indescribably humorous. It was Mirth's own countenance in the act of laughing. The wall of one side was literally covered with portraits of men, animals, and strange pictures born of mad conceit. Here a death's head grinned at us. Below it a culprit was hanging from the gallows-bar, the face brutal, contorted, and the dangling body horribly flexed, — a dreadful bit of realistic work to haunt the memory and terrify sleep. In juxtaposition to it was a foundering ship, in the act of going down, the stern already under water, the prow lifted, and men clinging to the rigging.

"This is horrible!" said the Judge as he stood gazing. "The man was mad."

"Perhaps," answered Mr. Pepperell. "But look on this side. Hold up your lights, all of you. I want you to get the full effect."

We turned with hands uplifted, holding the lights high.

A canvas. And on the canvas the portrait of a woman. A woman in the full bloom of her loveliness. A brunette. The "Queen of the Creoles" she might have been when living, so rich, so ripe, so perfect was she. A vision of female possibility such as floats in the air before the eyes of the opium eater, as he lies half asleep in his sensuous heaven. Her head was small, shapely, and crowned with braids of glossy blackness. Her eyes were large, long, softly black, like the star-lighted dusk of a tropical night. Her lips were full, curved, slightly parted. The rounded neck and shoulders were modestly revealed, and the bare, perfectly modeled arms were lifted as to a loved one coming to their embrace. The face was full of fire, of passion, of expectancy. But, oh, horrible, horrible sight! *A dagger was driven to its hilt in her breast!*

"My God!" exclaimed the Judge. "This is too dreadful!" and he turned his back to the picture shudderingly.

"What do you make of it?" I asked, as I turned away from the same impulse. "Judge, what do you make of it?"

"Make of it?" he responded. "It is perfectly clear that that lovely woman was his wife, his love, or his mistress, and she was murdered in the very act of embracing him, and his awful punishment or fate drove him mad. This cave of his is an artistic bedlam, a mad painter's hell."

"I think," said Colonel Goffe, "he murdered her himself. He caught her in the act of unfaithfulness, and his hand drove that dagger home. The remembrance of it made him mad."

"Gentlemen," said Mr. Pepperell, "seat yourselves around this table. I wish to show you something. I spent a night in this cave, and I discovered some of its secrets."

"Why did you not stay and find them all out?" I asked. "You certainly had made a good start."

"Simply because I was afraid to stay longer — afraid

I should go mad myself if I did," he answered. "Look

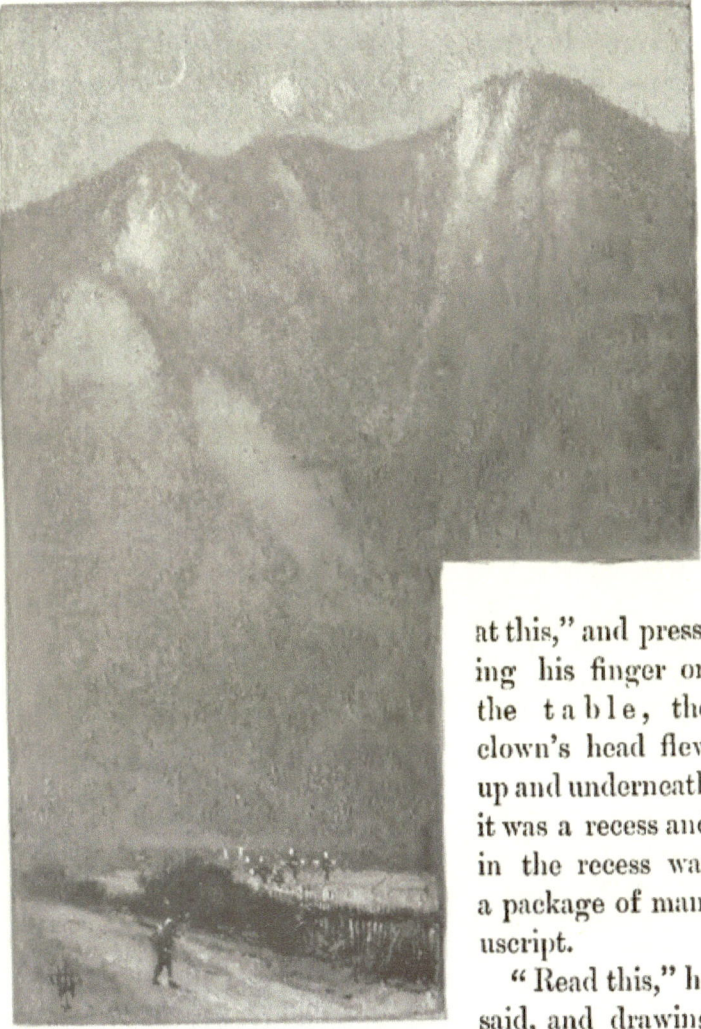

at this," and pressing his finger on the table, the clown's head flew up and underneath it was a recess and in the recess was a package of manuscript.

"Read this," he said, and drawing out a leaf of the manuscript, he handed it to me.

It was a beautiful bit of artistic embellishment.

The text was delicately printed. Each capital letter was ornamented with some lovely or quaint device, while around the sheet was a border of vines and flowers beautifully executed. It was a metrical composition. Here it is: —

FORGOTTEN.

I passed the gates of Death, and in the light
I looked to see those whom I thought to meet.
But none were there. I knew no Angel face.
They who had gone before, yea even those
Who with love's dread of parting from the loved
Were torn from out my arms, had found new loves,
And now were fixed forever in new lives.
They had forgotten me. And there I stood
At Heaven's gate, and saw that I must take
The old search up to find some faithful one
To serve and love me as I had been loved.
I could not do it. Nay, I was too faint,
Too tired, from the old seeking, out of which
I had just come. I turned, and from the gate
Called Beautiful I downward went unto
Those other gates, within which lies a land
All cold and dim, to which those go at wish
Who have lost all, and find — forgetfulness.
Into this land, cold, dim, and dark, I went,
That being thus forgot I might forget.

"That's a strange thing," said the Judge.
"Here's another," remarked Mr. Pepperell, and he handed me the second sheet. "Read that." I did as requested, and read: —

A VISIT.

Beyond the glorious gates I met a soul
That on the earth had been betrothed to me.
She loved me with the love of time and sense,
The love which women give to mortal men,
And out of which come births, and later, graves.
In joy I ran to her with arms outstretched —
Outstretched to fold her in my fond embrace,
And with warm lips press kisses on her mouth
As I had done in the dear days below.
But she with startled eyes stared full at me,
And speechless stood, as if struck dumb with fright
At sight so strange she knew not what it meant.

I spoke her name. That name which was to me
As sweet as cry of new-born babe to her
Who in her pain hears that sure sign of life,
And panting feels the joy of motherhood.
But she stood coldly still, nor gave a sign
That she remembered either name or me.
A new name had been given her above.
In death she lost one life, another found,
And what she found was not as what she lost.
She knew not me nor any thing that was.
And so I turned and gladly journeyed down
To earth and human life and its warm loves.

"This is uncanny business, this reading a dead man's private papers without legal permission," remarked the Judge, after we had sat in silence a moment. "I feel as if I were one of a party engaged in robbing a grave."

"Here it is! here it is!" suddenly exclaimed Mr. Pepperell, as he lifted a small package neatly folded from the bottom of the recess. "Read this, Mr. Murray, and then I will show you something that will startle you," and he passed a portion of the package over to me.

I took it from his hand, and, smoothing it out carefully on the table, proceeded to read the following strange communication.

THE LAST WILL AND TESTAMENT
OF
ONE WHOSE NAME IS HIDDEN, WHO ALONE KNOWS HIMSELF, AND WHO IS KNOWN ONLY
UNTO GOD
AS
THE HERMIT OF FRASER CAÑON.
I AM MAD.

"The proof of it is on these walls. What drove me mad is also on these walls. I killed her. Guilt is on us both. Her portrait. Love. Conscience. Here have I lived eighteen hundred years with her in torment. The ecstasies of heaven and the agonies of hell have been mine. Ha! ha! ha! ha!

"Yes. I am mad, but I am cunning. My mind never stops. It spins like a buzz-wheel. I have more than mortal power. I can live without food. I have clairvoyant sight. I can see the bottom of the Fraser. It is solid gold. I can hear through a mountain.

"I leave my body and visit worlds. I come back and enter it again. I can become incorporeal at will. I am an unit of pure consciousness, a receptive essence, an atom of universal apprehension. Amen.

" Let him who would know a mystery read. Let him who would solve it obey. Let him who dare, put his ear to the breast of the woman and listen."

" Judge Doe," said Mr. Pepperell, " go to the canvas. Put your ear to it and listen. What do you hear ? "

" Water," answered the Judge in astonishment. " The sound of running water as it plunges over a distant fall and pours softly down among stones," and he returned to his seat on the bench.

I read on.

" Have you listened ? Has the heart of the mountain told you its secret ? Have you heard the river that pours from under the Glacier ? Do you know that its sands are pure gold ; that all the gold in the Fraser comes down that stream ? I have seen. I have digged my grave on its bank. I shall sleep, when I die, in a chamber of gold. He who finds me might purchase the world. He will have all that man craves but one thing. He will not have love. Hue ! hue !

" ' He is mad,' " you who read say. So I am. I know it. But I am cunning. The hidden I found, and what I found I have hidden. I mock you. I laugh from where I am hidden. My eyes are on you. I am near, a foot away, a yard distant, a span off. Why don't you find me ? I am grinning at you at this moment. Ho ! ho ! "

"This is the raving of madness," I exclaimed. "I will read no more of the trash," and I threw the sheet on the table.

"Read to the end," cried Mr. Pepperell. "Read to the end of it, then I will show you something." Thus urged I read on.

"Are you wise? Are you brave? Are you cunning? Can you read a riddle that is plain? Then read the riddle that I write on the page that comes next."

"Here it is," cried Mr. Pepperell. "Here is the page that comes next, and on it the madman's riddle. Who can read it?"

A white sheet of paper, blankly white, that was all!

"What can you make of it?" It was Mr. Pepperell that put the question.

"Make of it? Nothing," I answered. "The man was mad."

"Wait a moment," he said. "Now look!" and lifting the blank sheet he held one of the candles under it a moment, and out of the white blankness started this sentence in letters red as blood.

"*He who calls these letters forth calls me from my grave! I am here with you!*"

And he dropped the sheet, across whose white surface stretched the red lines, upon the table.

We were on our feet like a flash — we three who had been sitting — on our feet, staring at the red letters, and at Mr. Pepperell, and at each other.

"Gentlemen," he said, "I got thus far a year ago and stopped. I was alone, remember, and I went out of this cave like a scared boy. But I am not alone to-night, and I stay it through, whether living or dead come. *Wait!*"

Was it a sound? Yes. It was a sound. The sound of one moving. Or was it the wind outside? Which? We held our breaths, listening. My heart sounded, as it beat in my breast, like a bell.

"The *canvas!* the *canvas! The woman is moving from the wall*," whispered the Judge hoarsely, and his face whitened to the color of chalk.

"This is nonsense," I said, pulling myself together stoutly, but my veins shriveled horribly, and the roots of my hair prickled in my scalp. "This is nonsense. It was the wind that did it," and I took a quick step forward and plucked the canvas with a jerk from the wall.

"*My God!*" It was the Judge's voice, and I heard him drop heavily on to the bench.

Back of the canvas stood a man! The madman himself! He was grinning insanely at us. And then, with a yell, he jumped full at me.

The table was overturned and every light extinguished.

We were not cowards, nor were we proof against such a shock. We acted, I presume, as any four men would naturally act whose senses had been thus suddenly and frightfully assaulted. We probably all yelled — I don't know — I know I did, as I jumped backward.

No man living could have stood unmoved such a revelation as the fall of that canvas made. The first thought that came to me, in the recoil of feeling and resultant return of sense, was for light. I felt for my matches and struck one mechanically. Mr. Pepperell kindled a fusee at the same instant. We lighted the candles, then the lantern, and for a moment stood looking at each other.

"See!" said Mr. Pepperell, as he pointed at the hole in the wall where the canvas had hung. It was an aperture in the side of the cavern; a large, oblong crevice in the cliff; the entrance to an interior passage which led deeper into the mountain.

"The riddle is solved any way, Mr. Pepperell," I said. "It was no ghost, but a man. He slipped as he jumped at me and struck the floor like a good solid human being. See. There is blood on the leg of the table. He hit it head on. The Hermit of Fraser Cañon is not dead. He is some escaped maniac. There is neither truth nor reason in his words or acts. That portrait is a lie. I don't believe he ever killed a woman or knew one that was killed. It is all a mad fancy of his, an insane delusion. What do you say, Colonel Goffe?"

"I — I don't believe he ever saw a woman in his life," said the Man from New Hampshire, dryly.

Strange that a single sentence neither wise nor very witty could affect us so happily, but that light remark of the Colonel acted as a sedative to our excited nerves. It brought us to our senses and normal condition. We were all ourselves again.

"Come," said the Judge. "Take the papers, Mr. Murray, and let us get out of this. Now that we know what this hole in the mountain is, I feel as if I were in the cell of some lunatic asylum. I will roll up the canvas and bring it along. It may help us discover who he is, or where his friends are. We must find the poor fellow if we rally the country and hunt him a month. It is plainly a case of insanity. He is a scholar and an artist, but overwork or some accident has driven him mad. It is a pity that the blow he received when he fell did n't stun him. It would have saved us much searching."

We did as the Judge suggested, and left the cave much relieved in our feelings and well content with the outcome of our strange adventure. But we had not come to the end of it. It was to be a night of surprises in fact, and the biggest one yet awaited us. For, as we drew near the flat ledge by the river, our camp-fire was burning brightly and a man was sitting by it bathing his face in some water.

It was the madman of the cave!

"Gentlemen," he said, addressing us as we approached, "I am an artist. I was sketching the Cañon by moonlight, and slipping, fell from a ledge. I got here with great difficulty. I do not remember how, for I struck my head against a sharp rock as I fell, and was partially stunned. I saw your camp-fire and crawled to it, and have taken the liberty of using one of your napkins to free my face from blood." This was spoken in a feeble voice, but accurately and rationally, and we instantly realized *that the blow he had received on his head as he jumped from the wall in the cave had restored him the use of his faculties, but left the time between his accident and his recovery a blank.*

"I am something of a surgeon," I said pleasantly, "and with your permission I will assist you to dress your wound," and I stepped to his side.

"You are very kind," he returned feebly, "very kind. I am grateful to God that the accident happened where it did, so near your camp, for I am feeling very weak, and I could not have crawled far. It was very foolish of me to spend a night alone in this Gorge, but its sublimities attracted me irresistibly. I feel it is destined to be noted the world over and I longed to be the first to put on canvas a moonlight and sunrise view of it. If this blow should prove serious," he continued more feebly, looking up into my face as I was carefully removing the hair from the edges of the gash, "my studio is in New Orleans. I have no relatives in this country but my betrothed," and here a slight flush came to his face. "My betrothed is a lady of that city, a Miss De Fontaine " —

"He has fainted," I said quietly. "Colonel Goffe, pour me a spoonful from your brandy flask."

CHAPTER XV.

FISH AND FISHING IN BRITISH COLUMBIA.

"The wealth of waters."

WE were all anglers, and our journey through British Columbia from the Shuswap Lake region to Vancouver was full of the keenest interest to us. We crossed the Columbia three hundred and seventy miles from Vancouver and entered Eagle Pass, which opens a way through the Gold Range, amid magnificent scenery. The valley is crowded with forest trees of giant size and of many varieties, which enrich the landscape with a splended arboreous appearance. The train rolls past lovely lakes, whose limpid waters stretch from base to base of the opposite mountains, and suggest to the tourist the beautiful lochs of Scotland. Beyond, are the great Shuswap Lakes, to which sportsmen from all parts of the continent are destined to come. At Sicamous, hunting parties can find accommodation and make their arrangements to enjoy the sport easily accessible from it as a starting point. The northward-going trails will conduct them to the caribou grounds, and to the south deer are found in abundance. Geese and ducks in their season abound in these lakes, whose great extent, beautiful shores, and accessibility commend them to the great fraternity of rod and gun. These bodies of inland water are fed by torrents and mountain streams, but are themselves tranquil, spreading out in placid reaches of great extent between the surrounding hills. Hundreds of miles of delightful boating can be found on these sheets of water, and the region around them is sufficiently settled and cultivated to easily furnish supplies. But the vast region around about these lakes is wholly unexplored or essentially so, and he who loves adventure in an unknown country can be accommodated to any extent. I hope these words will prompt many young and vigorous sportsmen to visit this charming and most attractive section of the continent, now made so easy of approach to them, and that from them I may, with all who love the outdoor life, receive spirited descriptions of this now almost wholly unvisited region.

The fish supply in the rivers and the coast waters of British Columbia is simply beyond estimate. No one who has not visited the country and seen with his own eyes can credit the most conservative statement of it.

In the Fraser River the tourist beholds a phenomenal condition to which there is no parallel in any other

section of the continent or in any other land. Only in the Columbia River does the Fraser find a rival. Five species of salmon frequent this river, and in incredible numbers. In many of the tributaries of it they literally pack the water solid from bank to bank.

The pools resembled purse nets when filled to the floats. In the Cañon of the Fraser in summer months millions of these fish can be seen from the car windows, packed into the eddies of the torrent stream or resting in the lee of rocks and projections, gathering strength for another rush upward through the tremulous water. It is a novel and picturesque sight for the tourist to gaze at. All along the banks, and on the projecting rocks stands the Indian, spear in hand; he suddenly rises to his full height, his sinewy arms, bared to the shoulder, gleaming in the sun, and from his nervous grasp is launched his salmon spear. Well aimed, surely sent! A struggle, a splashing, and a glistening fish is lifted from the water and lies, silvery white, on the brown ledge at the spearman's feet.

First of all in the spring comes up the silver salmon, a beautiful fish to look upon and often of magnificent size, varying from five to seventy pounds. Their run begins in March and lasts until the last of June. Then come a small species, but greatly prized, averaging about five pounds in weight. Their flesh is brightly pink. This is the kind that is most sought for canning purposes. They run from June until August. Next in order is an excellent variety, much esteemed, averaging some seven pounds in weight. Then comes an anomaly among salmon, the "noan" or "humpbacked," whose run lasts from August into winter, but which visits the river but once in two years. And last of all, in September the "hookbill" appears, a fish that weighs as high as twenty-five pounds, and disappears at Christmas. Such is the list of the Fraser River salmon and their characteristics,

and no party of ladies and gentlemen could have a more novel and enjoyable experience than they might obtain by camping a week or a month near the Great Cañon of the Fraser River at Yale, in the months of July, August, and September, when the gold seekers are washing the sand on the bars, and the Indians are spearing salmon in the whirlpools and rapids of the Cañon. If a party camped amid such scenery and novel surroundings did not find rare enjoyment, it would be because of something inherently depraved or cross-grained in their constitutions. I speak with deliberation when I say that I know not one locality on the continent I would so quickly select for a party of intelligent and congenial people to camp a few weeks as the Cañon of the Fraser. It is the one spot of all others for the amateur photographer and the artist to visit, and it would be a real benefit to the lovers of nature in its sublime and strange aspects to have put within their reach pictorial presentations of this awful chasm.

In addition to the salmon, the fresh-water streams and lakes abound with game fish. Whitefish, salmon trout, brook trout, and big lake trout are found in abundance everywhere. A rodsman can find prime sport wherever he goes through the province, whether among the inland lakes and rivers or along the coast waters. There is no other stretch of coast on the globe along which, and in the rivers flowing into it, so many varieties of edible fish are caught as off the shore and in the streams of British Columbia. Beside the salmon and trout are the halibut, the cod, the mackerel, the haddock, the rock cod, the flounders, and that delicious tidbit of marine delicacy, the oolahan or candle fish. This little fish is of the size of a sardine and has a flavor peculiarly its own, so piquant and delicate as to justify its claim of being, *par excellence*, an epicurean morsel. Prepared for the plate fresh from the water, it is exceedingly delicious, while its oil is said to be preferable to cod-liver oil for medicinal purposes. These fish are supposed to come from far northern waters, and they come in numberless quantities. They enter the Fraser about the first of May, and swarm up its current as bees swarm in a hive. The herrings of the coast are equally numberless. These are somewhat smaller than those found along the shores of Labrador and the British Isles, but as food are fully as good as those caught in the waters of the Atlantic. It is only when one adds to the fish supply of eastern Canada the even larger one of British Columbia, that the value of the Canadian fisheries to herself and the world can be realized.

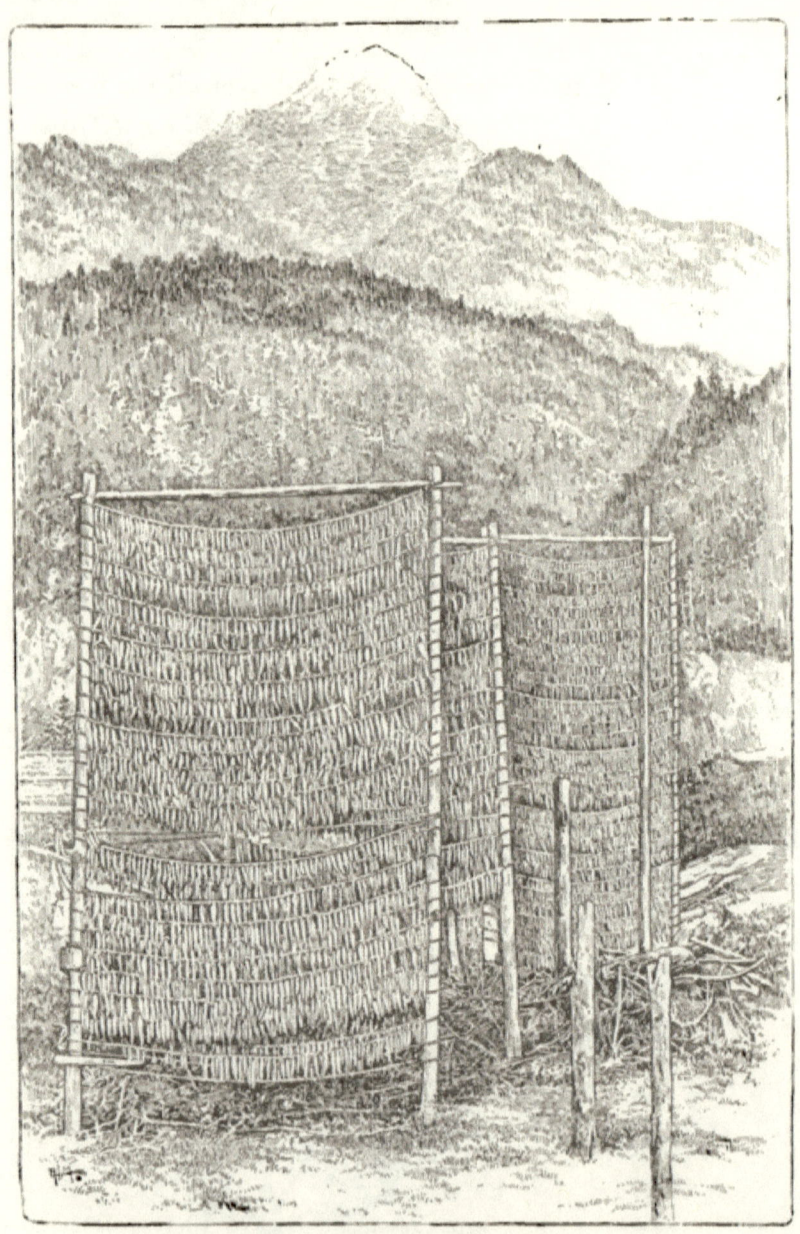

DRYING CANDLE FISH.

CHAPTER XVI.

VANCOUVER.

WHAT San Francisco was once, Vancouver is now, — an oak within an acorn, a vital root well placed, but only just sprouted; but all the conditions of a great city are here, and here a great city is to be. Colonel Goffe, I will buy this corner lot if you will take the opposite one, or I will toss for the choice. What say you?" It was Mr. Pepperell who spoke.

"Judge, you pitch for us," replied the Man from New Hampshire, laconically. Up went the cent, and as it came down and rolled curving through the dust, the two speculators chased it, laughing like boys, to see who had won the lot on which we were standing.

"Well, well," exclaimed the Judge, as the two men scuffled over the penny, "you are genuine Yankees, and you type both the shrewdness and recklessness of our countrymen, who buy bits of the continent as brokers do stocks, and purchase locations as gamblers do chips. One might fancy that you think you are standing on the site of a future Chicago by the way you are acting."

"You old Areopagite," exclaimed Mr. Pepperell, as he wrestled with the Colonel for the token. "We don't think any such thing, but we know that fifty thousand people will have their homes here on this peninsula within twenty years, and we know that two big buildings will stand on these corner lots inside of a year, for we will build them ourselves."

"How do you figure that out?" retorted the Judge. "This isn't Yankee land, remember, and Canadians move slowly."

"Judge Doe," responded Mr. Pepperell, as he let go his hold on the Colonel, and sobered down, "we have been in this city two days. The Colonel and I have been canvassing this place, and we have sized up the outlook to a shaving. The conditions which make for success are all here. In the first place the men who have founded this city have the right stuff in them. There isn't a slow drop of blood in their veins. They are not a gang of mere speculators. They are gentlemen of substance and character, and they have come to stay. They have put in their money, thou-

TOSSING FOR CORNER LOTS.

sands and thousands of it. Look at these solid blocks of stone and brick, at that opera house, at that hotel which must have cost nigh on to a quarter of a million; look at their gas works and water works, their steam fire-engines, their miles of paved streets and sidewalks, that magnificent driving park, with its splendid boulevard clear around it, their boating club and athletic grounds, those lines of wharves and yonder huge steamships loading and unloading at them. 'Boomers' and land gamblers don't do such work as these men have done here. They are Americanized Canadians, sir, the best city builders on the continent, for they build with the solidity of the English and the celerity of the Yankee. Colonel Goffe, you villain you, which lot am I to take? If there was the difference of a dollar between them, I would have you up before the peripatetic court that travels around with us and compel you to disgorge."

Vancouver — the city, I mean, not the huge island of that name lying thirty miles out in the Pacific, and stretching three hundred miles northward like a great natural breakwater, as it is, along the coast — Vancouver is a city site, literally hewn out of the solid forest, which, with its gigantic timber trees, makes the sea front of British Columbia. And what a forest it is! An Eastern born man knows nothing of it unless he has crossed the continent and actually seen it, nor can he conceive of it, for the woods of the East supply him with no standard of comparison; even the largest pines of Michigan give him only a hint of what this mighty forest of the Pacific coast really is. The trees

stand from two hundred and fifty to three hundred feet in height, and so densely packed together that progress among them is absolutely impossible. Large tracts are actually destitute of game because of the density of this forest growth. Here is a lumber supply for the whole world for centuries to come. As a source of future wealth to the country, its value cannot be overestimated. The market for this lumber is found in Japan, in China, in Australia, in San Francisco, in local development, and in that measureless demand which the prairies, only five hundred miles to the east, will make upon it when they are peopled with their millions, as they soon will be, and cities like Minneapolis and St. Paul and Duluth stand on the great water-courses which thread the Mackenzie Basin with

possibilities of inland commerce, and steel pathways connect them with Lake Superior, or straight eastward, south of James's Bay, with the Saguenay, at Chicoutimi. Place the minerals, the fish, the coal, and the forests of British Columbia in the one scale, and how many millions of dollars, do you fancy, you will have to pile into the opposite scale to bring the bar level? No intelligent American ever visited this Pacific province of Canada, and saw what it contains, and did not grind his teeth as he recalled how the miserable, blundering, partisan politics of the Polk *régime*, lost it to the Great Republic. Let any statesman who loves his country and is proud of its vast geographical extent and future greatness, take a map of the Pacific coast and see what a gap this one province of the Dominion makes in its western sea line, — longer by far than the Atlantic coast from the Florida Keys to Cape Breton. And, verily, what did the Polk administration do to make amends to the American people for this criminal blunder? Had Polk's secretary of state secured British Columbia for us as Seward secured Alaska, — well, things would now be a good deal different from what they are, would n't they? The Republic has been taxed pretty heavily to support her petty politicians and miserable partisan politics, truly.

Out of such a forest, as we said, a site for Vancouver City has been hewn. It cost three hundred dollars per acre to merely fell and burn the gigantic growth. When we arrived, only two trees were still standing, and they were burning like a blast furnace inside their hollow trunks. They were nearly three hundred feet in height and measured between thirty and forty feet in circumference. For one hundred and fifty feet they rose like mammoth pillars of wood, straight as a plumb line, bare of branch or knot. Our artist sketched them on the spot only an hour before they fell with a sweep, a rush, and a roar of sound as if the columns which uphold the sky had slipped from their bases and a section of heaven had dropped suddenly — a vast ruin — to the earth. The earth trembled to the shock of their overthrow, the air groaned, and as the roar of their fall rolled across the level water of Burrard's Inlet, through the still air, the mountains beyond sent back the murmurs of their regret. Alas, that life must forever feed its growth on death, and human progress advance only over the ruins of the perfect!

CEDAR, VANCOUVER PARK: 50 FEET IN CIRCUMFERENCE.

They fell, and the saws went at them. How their senseless, hungry, cruel teeth ate into and destroyed the majesty of their sublime proportions! We turned away, from a sense of pain and sheer vexation. In the evening the Judge and I crept up through the debris and heavy semi-tropical undergrowth to the crown of the hill on which they had stood. The warm evening air was filled with a ruddy glow, for a hundred giant stumps were still feebly gasping forth fire. We lighted two resinous torches and counted the rings which would give us the measure of their age.

"*Six hundred and seven-*

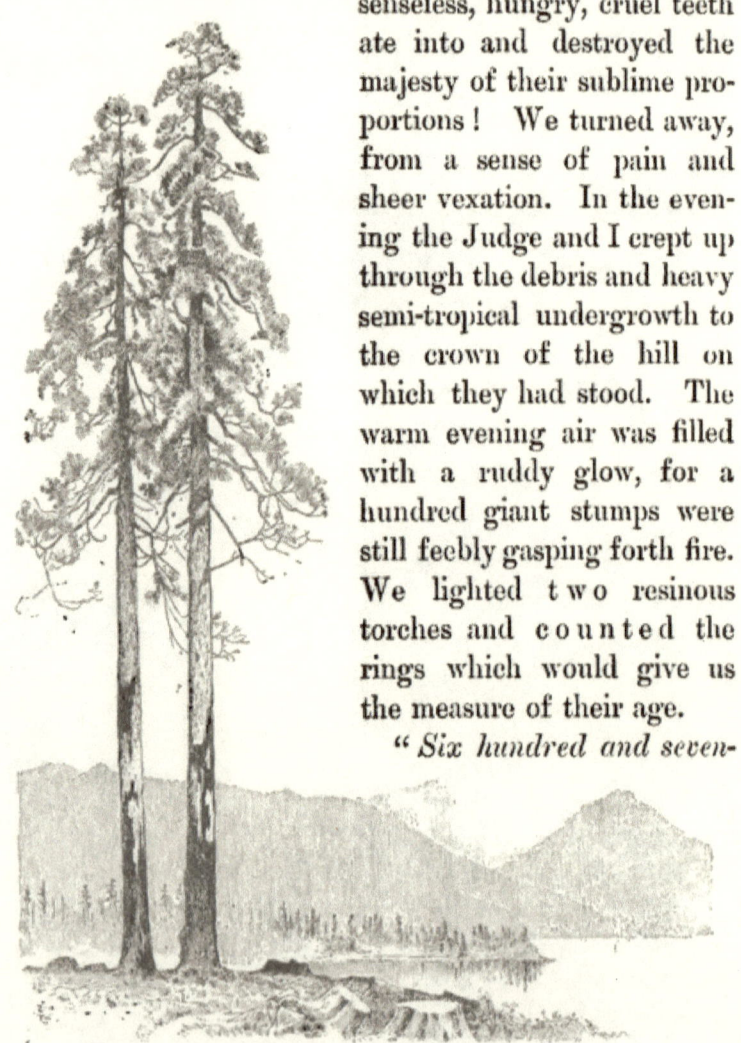

ty-four years old!" gasped the Judge, and he dropped his torch to the ground. "My God! these trees were older than the landing of Columbus, older than Magna Charta, older than the first translation of the Bible into English, and last week they stood with a thousand years of life ahead of them, and these men of Vancouver have levelled them to the earth with as little sense of what they were doing as the Vandals had when they overturned the immortal sculptures of Rome, and trampled the triumphs of art under the hoofs of their chargers! It is simply brutal. But the trees will have long and sure revenge."

"How is that?" I queried, as I flung my torch away in rage at what had been done, for I shared the indignation of my companion. "How will these thoughtless people be punished for this wanton deed?"

"Mr. Murray," cried the Judge in reply, "Boston would give a million of dollars to have two such trees, growthful and strong with six centuries of growth and ten centuries of life ahead of them on her Common. What would London give for two such monuments? What Paris? Had these Vancouver men had the reverence or wit to have set apart a space six hundred feet across for a small park on this knoll, — the very centre and crown of their city, that is to be, — they would have made it the Mecca of thousands upon thousands of visitors each year. That railroad there could have afforded to pay a million of dollars to have kept these two gigantic trees, these majestic monuments of past centuries, built up from the soil, the air, and the sunshine, by the Lord, standing here. There is not a sculpture, shaft, or fresco in Rome, that can compare with these trees as they stood but yesterday

SPRUCE TREE, VANCOUVER PARK: 43 FEET IN CIRCUMFERENCE.

in their attractiveness to the eyes and the imagination of men. These trees thus preserved would have made their city one of the noted cities of the world. Every pen that came hither would have written of them; every pencil have sketched them; every brush made them the foreground of this magnificent view; every tongue told of them to listening ears far away. The Bank of England put at their disposal could not buy for them such an advertisement as these two trees gave them free of cost. And now they lie in these hot ashes lost to the world forever, burning as if they were an offense to the eye, a stench to the senses, a collection of offal. What a pity, what a loss! Come, let us get away from this spot. The air is filled with the reproach of the centuries that look upon their highest artistic result as despised and rejected of men. I shall always think of Vancouver as I should of Rome if St. Peter's were destroyed by a mob."

It was not until we had returned to the hotel, and the Judge had seated himself at a table in the supper room, that he regained his wonted spirits. The vast and elegant hostelry was filled with happy noises, for a band of stringed instruments was playing and fifty couples were whirling through the mazes of a waltz, while the low buzz of conversation in the wide corridors, and now and then a peal of merry laughter mingled pleasantly with the strains of music. It was in truth a bright and animated scene, and one most suggestive withal.

"This is a most astonishing spectacle," remarked the Judge, as we sat on one of the wide verandas of the great house, gazing through the wide open windows at the merry dancers whirling around the large hall within. "Two years ago this city site was covered with a mighty forest, so dense that even a bear could scarcely thread a way through it, and now behold what is here, — blocks of brick and stone, wide streets, pavements echoing to the tread of a thousand feet, gas, electric lights, green swarded lawns, fountains, flowers, and a fashionable hop in a hotel that cost a quarter of a million of money. That train rolling into the depot yonder has two coaches in it filled with Bostonians. Massachusetts Bay sends its greeting to Burrard's Inlet. What would not San Francisco have given for rail connection with the Atlantic, when her census counted only seven thousand. And what an impetus such a connection would have given to her development. Mr. Pepperell, this is an age of enchantment, as you say. The wand of measureless power is being waved over this continent, and no man can predict the rate of its progress in civilization. This in truth is the day when old men can dream dreams and our young men behold visions. We Americans and our Canadian neighbors must join hands and keep them joined in strong fraternal clasp. We are brethren. The continent geographically is a unit, and we who shape its development in wealth and population must shape it along the lines of affectionate union. The Lord of it will smite us in his wrath if we do otherwise. The moonlight on yonder mountains and the music might well keep us from sleep, but we must start fresh as boys for Victoria to-morrow, and hence the couch must be honored.

THE BALL.

Gentlemen, I wish you good night, restful sleep, and pleasant dreams." And we strolled away to our rooms.

Dear old, courteous, wise, happy-hearted Judge — a gentleman, that highest of titles — thy face is a picture which the memory of three men will keep until all bright pictures fade and all sweet earthly things are forgotten, if they ever shall be. Who knows?

CHAPTER XVII.

THE PARTING AT VICTORIA.

"THESE are not Indians," said the Judge, as we stood on the bridge at Victoria, looking down upon a dozen Siwash canoes filled with their strange looking owners. "These are not Indians," he repeated, "they are Mongolians."

"And look at their boats," exclaimed Mr. Pepperell; "they have n't the least resemblance to a birch-bark canoe. They suggest the Chinese junks, rather. Observe their length, narrowness, and high, projecting prows."

"Not a bad boat for a heavy sea," I remarked. "That one putting off from the shore must be forty

SIWASH CANOES.

feet long, and with her twenty paddles, and well steered, would climb safely over a mighty big swell, for she sits as lightly on the water as if made of bamboo."

"Look there," cried Mr. Pepperell, pointing to a boat just coming into sight from under the bridge. "That is the Medicine Man of the tribe, and his wife."

"Well," said the Colonel, "I am a great admirer of the ladies, but I must confess that Mrs. Medicine Man does n't impress me as being a great beauty. What do you say, Judge?"

"This is a very strange spectacle," responded the Judge; "a very strange spectacle, indeed. I have seen many queer looking people, but I have never seen a more singular looking folk than these Siwash Indians. Ethnologically, I don't know where to place them."

It was a strange spectacle in truth. The river was covered with their long, light, narrow craft. Some were shooting rapidly along in straight courses, some drifting with the tide, others grouped side by side. The tribe were preparing to move off on a fishing excursion, and the low soft murmur of many voices filled the air. All was activity, but there was no bustle, no confusion, no sharp word of command or loud calls. A pretty sight they made as they moved away, a long procession of strange looking boats, each trailing exactly in line of the one ahead of it, the paddles rising and falling in concert, the blue water beneath them and their high-colored blankets showing brightly in the sun.

"*Bon voyage! Bon voyage!*" cried the Judge to them as the last canoe passed from under the bridge on which we stood, and glided away.

The steersman, an old wrinkled Siwash, who was standing in the stern of the craft, looked up at the Judge and smiled; at least his leathery face was suddenly cut up into wrinkles, and his toothless gums showed between his parted lips.

"That wasn't a bad grin, Judge," said the Man from New Hampshire. "Ethnologically I should place that old specimen of Siwash antiquity halfway between a low-bred Mongolian and a high-bred ape. Darwin should have come to Victoria for his 'connecting link.'"

Victoria is well worth seeing. The tourist can find entertainment there. He can pick up a quantity of interesting curios and not be swindled in so doing. We four spent the day, happy-hearted as boys in their first journey from home. Life brings many losses to us, as we live, but none greater than the loss of the boyish eye and heart. He who keeps these, long after his head is white, has prolonged the finest pleasures of life. What a day we four gray-headed boys had at this most western city of our race, thrust out from the continent like a picket in front of an encamped army.

We visited the fish market and saw how royally the city was fed by the sea, — salmon, trout, halibut, haddock, cod, the delicious oolahan or candle fish, and a dozen sorts, some of them new to us. In one market we found a huge octopus or devil-fish suspended for advertisement, a ghastly creature, with tentacled arms nine feet in stretch. The Italians and Chinese eat them. And the marketman assured us that "octopus steak was n't bad eating."

"Let me get out of this place," cried the Judge, shudderingly, "or I shall not eat a mouthful of dinner to-day."

"That devil-fish," said the Man from New Hampshire, "does make a man feel a little creepy inside, does n't it, Judge?"

We visited stores where furs and skins are bought of the Indians, and the warehouses where they are packed. What a collection of furs we saw! And

there all, save one of us, saw for the first time that finest, rarest fur of the world, the magnificent sea otter. Did you ever see one, madame? No? What pleasure you have awaiting you ahead. Wait until your white fingers can feel their way through the fur of a sea otter! Ah, me, beaver will never content you after that. We visited all the pawnshops, and in them discovered many curious bits brought from the four corners of the earth, — Japan, China, Australia, New Zealand, the two Indies, the Arctic Ocean, Mexico, and Palestine, all had contributed to the unique collections. Strange pipes, antique arms, nuggets of gold, pearls, rude coins, Indian armor deftly quilted. Grotesque masks, flaming

head-dresses, and skins from every furred animal of the continent. In one shop we were shown an Oriental ruby, the iridescent splendors of which were beyond all conception.

"A stone," said the Judge, "to be set in the gate of heaven." That describes it.

Then there were specimens of Indian workmanship, carved plates and salvers of jet black stone, valued at a hundred dollars each; birds and fish and national banners fashioned in pure gold, exquisitely wrought; baskets, woven from the fibres of roots, in which water can be boiled; juvenile toys in wicker in loveliest of colors; bows and arrows from polished bone, tipped with stone or steel, dipped in deadliest poisons; gambling sticks and conjurers' robes, and a hundred and one odd things, novel and most instructive to civilized people, — how much we saw and how much we enjoyed it all. What a day we four tourists had at Victoria!

Thus pleasantly passed the day, and pleasantly it drew to its close. We were standing on the battery south of the city, as it declined. In front of us the water stretched away, level as a floor, — a wide emerald plain with the shifting colors of sunset playing over it, coming and going, deepening and fading. To the east and south we saw the snowy peak of Mount Baker. To the west the red sun was going slowly downward, carrying all its splendors into the great ocean whose farther waves were rolling in white far up on orient beaches. We had come to the end of our journey. It had been, as the Judge had predicted at the start, a happy one to us all, and with happy hearts we were ready to turn our faces toward our distant homes. What a revelation it had been to us! The Judge was to take boat to the Golden Gate, and we escorted him on board, anxious to be with one whose intelligence and urbanity had ministered so much to our entertainment as we journeyed, to the last moment.

"Gentlemen," said the Judge, "this winter you must all come to San Francisco, and be my guests; we will do California, Mexico, and Arizona, together. Next summer, Mr. Pepperell, you shall be our host for a

week, and we will eat beans with you at the Somerset Club. By that time we can buy tickets through to Yokohama and Hong Kong, and see the West and the East, both hemispheres, and the youngest and oldest civilization in the world side by side in one trip. Such opportunities of pleasure and profit mankind have never enjoyed before since the race was born. What say you, gentlemen, shall we go over and see the land of the Celestials next summer?"

"Judge Doe," answered Colonel Goffe, "when the golden sands of California call, the rich soil of New Hampshire will respond. I will buy a railroad ticket to any spot in this world, or the next, you may suggest, provided it gives me your company. Only let us have

THE PARTING.

Jack Osgood along with us, for he and I are bound to pick up a little paying investment, occasionally, wherever we go, unless different arrangements prevail there from what we have in New Hampshire," and then, lifting his beaver, the tall, gray-headed Yankee, born trader and traveller, type of that energy and courage which have threaded their strength and color into the warp and woof of the continent, and whose shrewd remarks and quaint, rippling humor had been half the life of the party, led us off in that royal old bit of loving sentiment, —

> "Should auld acquaintance be forgot
> And never brought to mind?
> Should auld acquaintance be forgot
> And days of auld Lang Syne?"

We sang it bravely, we four gray-headed men, standing on the deck of the steamer with the purple light of the early gloaming upon us. Nor did we sing it far as a quartette; for on the deck were other wanderers like ourselves, far from friends and home, and among them a group of Scottish immigrants, red-haired, rough-bearded, and who were as responsive to the first note of the grand old stave as powder is to the spark, and whose strong voices, with their broad accent, joined in with such a rush and roar of sound as the Campbells brought with them when they charged into Lucknow.

At the close? Well, there were tears in our eyes. You need n't laugh, young man. Wait till you get on toward your evening, and know what home, country, and partings mean. You will never laugh then at the noble moistening of eyes. As I came off the boat I ran against a big Australian who had just parted at the gate with his wife.

"Beg pardon," he said, "I did n't see you coming."

"I beg your pardon," I returned, "I did n't see you either."

Then we looked at each other, and we both saw why we had not seen!

WORKS BY W. H. H. MURRAY.

DAYLIGHT LAND.

The Experiences, Incidents, and Adventures, Humorous and Otherwise, which befell Judge JOHN DOE, *Tourist, of San Francisco;
Mr.* CEPHAS PEPPERELL, *Capitalist, of Boston; Colonel*
GOFFE, *the Man from New Hampshire, and divers
others, in their Parlor-Car Excursion over
Prairie and Mountain; as recorded and
set forth by* W. H. H. MURRAY.

Superbly illustrated with 150 cuts in various colors by the best artists.

CONTENTS: Introduction — The Meeting — A Breakfast — A Very Hopeful Man — The Big Nepigon Trout — The Man in the Velveteen Jacket — The Capitalist — Camp at Rush Lake — Big Game — A Strange Midnight Ride — Banff — Sabbath among the Mountains — Nameless Mountains — The Great Glacier — The Hermit of Frazer Cañon — Fish and Fishing in British Columbia — Vancouver — Parting at Victoria.

8vo, 338 pages.   Unique paper boards, $2.50; cloth, $3.50; cloth, full gilt, $4.00.

Mr. Murray has chosen the northwestern side of the continent for the scene of this book; a region of country which is little known by the average reader, but which in its scenery, its game, and its vast material and undeveloped resources supplies the author with a subject which has not been trenched upon even by the magazines, and which he has treated in that lively and spirited manner for which he is especially gifted. The result is a volume full of novel information of the country, humorous and pathetic incidents, vivid descriptions of its magnificent scenery, shrewd forecasts of its future wealth and greatness when developed, illustrated and embellished with such lavishness and artistic elegance as has never before been attempted in any similar work in this country.

The Critic, in a recent issue, receiving the illustrated edition of Daudet's "Robert Helmont," says, "We wonder if the time will ever come when the creations of our own writers will be interpreted with equal sympathy," and, in view thereof, we would respectfully submit the above book to the critics and the public at large in evidence that the long-desired time has now arrived.

**CUPPLES AND HURD, PUBLISHERS,
BOSTON, MASS.**

For other books, see next page.

ADIRONDACK TALES.

By W. H. H. MURRAY.

Illustrated. 12mo, 300 pages, $1.25.

CONTENTS.

John Norton's Christmas.
Henry Herbert's Thanksgiving.
A Strange Visitor.
Lost in the Woods.
A Jolly Camp.
Was it Suicide?
The Gambler's Death.
The Old Beggar's Dog.
The Ball.
Who was he?

 Comment on these seem almost superfluous, so well are they known and appreciated. The quaintness and upright sturdiness of John Norton, the weird "Strange Visitor," the solemnity of "The Gambler's Death" in the very heart of nature, the deep pathos of "The Old Beggar's Dog," the spontaneous jollity of "The Ball," the mystery of "Was it Suicide?" and "Who was he?" all appeal most powerfully to our many-facetted nature. And over all, and in all, and through all, is the charm of Mr. Murray's individuality expressed in his unique style. Critics have in vain endeavored to define that quality in a book which renders it appreciated by every reader; we all know that it exists, but it eludes all effort to crystallize it into a phrase.

 These stories are full of that subtle charm, and their daily increasing popularity abundantly testifies to the fact.

ADVENTURES IN THE WILDERNESS;

Or, Camp Life in the Adirondacks.

By W. H. H. MURRAY.

Illustrated. 12mo, $1.25.

CONTENTS.

INTRODUCTION.

CHAP.
1. The Wilderness.
2. The Nameless Creek.
3. Running the Rapid.
4. The Ball.
5. Loon-Shooting in a Thunder-Storm.

CHAP.
6. Crossing the Carry.
7. Rod and Reel.
8. Phantom Falls.
9. Jack-Shooting in a Foggy Night.
10. Sabbath in the Woods.
11. A Ride with a Mad Horse in a Freight Car.

 This book, originally published twenty years ago, is now republished in response to repeated general inquiries. Many will remember its immense popularity at the time of its first issue, when it practically directed the attention of the American public to an unknown section of their country; and earned for the author the sobriquet of "Adirondack" Murray.

 Distinguished as an orator, he then introduced to the reading world those wonderful gifts of descriptive writing, genuine humor and pathos, and complete sympathy with Nature in her various moods, which have now become so well known, and this work will ever be found fresh and breezy, picturesque and amusing, besides being one of the best guide-books extant to the wonderful and beautiful region of which it treats.

A Brief Biography
OF
W. H. H. MURRAY.

W. H. H. MURRAY was born in 1840 at Guilford, Connecticut. His earliest characteristic was love of books. He was born with a passion for knowledge. Before entering college and during his course he studied poetry and *belles-lettres* under Fitz-Greene Halleck, the poet, with whom he was a great favorite.

Mr. Murray was graduated from Yale in the class of '62. While at Yale, he was, above all else, a reader of books. His memory was extraordinary, and he seemed incapable of forgetting. A book once read was his at call forever. The great object of all his reading and study was his native tongue. He mastered English literature from beginning to date. He read everything; he read critically, and he never forgot what he read.

After his graduation he studied theology at East Windsor and under private teachers. His first engagement as preacher was as assistant to Dr. Edward Hatfield, D. D., New York City. This engagement terminated with Dr. Hatfield's resignation. He then served at Washington, Litchfield Co., Conn.; Greenwich, Conn.; Meriden, Conn.; at Park Street Church, Boston, seven years; Music Hall, Independent Congregational Church, three years, — fifteen years in all of steady, continuous service. From preacher to a small country congregation, his abilities and laborious studentship lifted him in six years to the leading pulpit in his denomination. In Boston, then as now the most literary city in the country, — whose pulpits and platforms had been for fifty years their pride, where eloquence of the highest order was familiar to all, — he remained for ten years, preaching to larger audiences every Sunday than any other preacher in the land, and, with one exception, as a *pulpit orator*, without a peer.

At the close of these fifteen years of service he retired from the ministry and the clerical profession, and entered upon a course of study best calculated in his opinion to fit him for authorship and the platform, broadly interpreted. He went abroad and made a thorough examination of English commercial methods, — her trade relations, her land system, and the tendency of her social and political forces. He remained a close observer of the great battle between Gladstone and D'Israeli, which ended in the triumph of the former, and then returned to his own country and entered upon a study of the resources and characteristics of this continent. To this investigation he devoted six years, and when he has completed his present extensive tour he will have personally visited, with the exception of Alaska, every representative section of the continent between Hudson's Bay and the Gulf of Mexico, and between Newfoundland and Vancouver. Few public or literary men, if any, have studied so thoroughly the resources of this continent, and the vast problems growing out of our continental development, as Mr. Murray. It is greatly to be desired, from every point of view, that one so well equipped for intelligent and candid discussion of these problems may be constrained by popular encouragement to do so.

In his self-command, in his reserve force, in the purity of his language, almost wholly Saxon, in quiet intensity and grace of style, in dignity of bearing, in clearness of statement, in the finish of his sentences, and in charm of his manner, he stands alone, although suggesting comparison, in one or more of these attributes, with many great writers.

Three years ago he began to read his now celebrated story, "How John Norton the Trapper kept his Christmas," and the people have insisted on hearing the author render this quaint, humorous, and pathetic bit of realism until it has already passed its three hundred and fiftieth delivery from the platform, and has been sold in book-form by thousands.

www.ingramcontent.com/pod-product-compliance
Lightning Source LLC
Chambersburg PA
CBHW030004240426
43672CB00007B/827